THE BOSTON MARATHON

The Boston Marathon

JOE FALLS

Macmillan Publishing Co., Inc.

NEW YORK

Collier Macmillan Publishers

LONDON

For Jerry Coyle and Bob Keiss,
two fast friends

Macmillan Publishing Co., Inc.
866 Third Avenue, New York, N.Y. 10022
Collier Macmillan Canada, Ltd.

Library of Congress Cataloging in Publication
Data

Falls, Joe.
    The Boston Marathon.

    1. Boston Marathon.   I.   Title.
GV1065.F34   796.4'26   76-50648
ISBN 0-02-537100-2

First Printing 1977
Printed in the United States of America

Beef Stew for 2,000 runners

245 lbs. potatoes
122 lbs. onions
190 lbs. carrots
 55 lbs. peas
750 lbs. beef chuck chunks
108 gallons beef gravy

Place in large pot and cook for a long time.

Courtesy Hugh Kindlan
Stouffer's
Prudential Tower

Contents

Foreword   ix

1   Why Boston?   1

2   "They Shall Rise From the Dust"   6

3   Marathon Madness   11

4   The Route: Trail of Terror   21

5   Boston: An Olympic Jinx   31

6   Jerry Nason Recalls the Marathon—and Tarzan Brown   35

7   The Bob & Jerry Show   46

8   "Mr. DeMarathon"   67

9   "Everybody Here's Seen Kelley!"   74

10 Monsieur Cote, the Fabulous Frenchman   80

11 Will Rodgers: Age of Innocence   87

12   *"Ladies, Start Your Engines!"*   92

13   *Our Not So Jolly Jock*   112

14   *Will Cloney: Man Behind the Scenes*   117

15   *Ted Corbitt: Man of Iron*   122

16   *Marathon Marriages*   129

17   *Scouting Report: Bad Eyes, Good Legs, Strong Heart*   135

18   *Alas, Poor Erich*   141

19   *Spinning Their Wheels*   145

20   *Man's Worst Friend*   149

21   *"Doctor, Can You Give Me a Hand With My Feet?"*   152

22   *And the Last Shall Be First*   158

23   *Marathon Champions*   163

     Index   195

Foreword

MAY 1976: A pleasant spring evening. Cool but not too cool. The sky is clear—that bright blue that makes Boston sparkle in the spring—and you can see the lights blazing over in Fenway Park where the Red Sox are in the midst of that terrible ten-game losing streak.

In my whole life I never dreamed I could get this close to Fenway Park—where I could see the back of that green wall and that giant net on top of it—and not go in. I always felt that if I had to spend the rest of my days in one place it might be in the press box at Fenway Park, looking out at that monstrous wall and that tantalizing net, waiting for another ball to go smashing up against that green barrier or hitting the net and sliding down out of sight. Did you know the Red Sox get to keep all of those balls—both from the game and from batting practice?

Now I didn't care. As a former baseball writer from Detroit, it meant nothing to me. I'd just gotten the pictures from the *Boston Globe*—Xerox copies of them—and as I hurried through the door of the Aegean Restaurant, a surpisingly nice Greek place in Kenmore Square, I couldn't wait to begin studying them. My publisher wanted thirty-five shots of the Boston Marathon for this book. I picked out eighty. How could I choose? How could I decide? They were filled with so much drama, so much emotion, so much pain— the agony and the ecstasy of it all—that it was just plain *impossible* to choose thirty-five of them. Maybe Fred Honig, my editor at Macmillan, could be talked into printing all eighty of them. Seventy? Sixty? How about fifty, Fred, old buddy?

I ordered the same for the third straight night—a glass of red wine, a salad with that beautiful feta cheese on top and three of the most delicious lamb chops this side of Greektown in Detroit. Now I was spreading the pictures out on the table.

Look at this one . . . snaking their way through the countryside. Here's Clarence H. DeMar (you always use the middle initial when you speak of this man). He's finishing in front of the Lenox Hotel. It's the 1920s. Or is it the 1930s? No matter. Clarence H. DeMar's picture would be one of the thirty-five finalists. Here's one of Will Rodgers tying his shoe . . .

"Watcha doin'?"

It was the waitress. She was standing there, smiling, holding my glass of wine and salad on a tray. Obviously, there was no room on the table for them. She saw my excitement—my elation—and she probably knew it was a special moment for me. She wasn't going to spoil it.

"Pictures?" she asked.

"Yeah."

"Of what?"

"The Boston Marathon."

"Oh."

I started putting them back into the manila folder. I felt a little stupid with the waitress standing there with no place to put the food.

"They're really something else," I said, trying to bide time while I cleaned up the mess.

"Do you know what I saw last year—do you know?"

She shook her head from side to side.

"I went out to Hopkinton—that's where they start the race. I went out there in the morning—they start it at noon. I went out there in a bus—I'm with the press and that's how we get out there."

Her smile broadened.

"Do you know something . . . I went out to Hopkinton, Massachusetts, and I saw two thousand people and there wasn't an unhappy face in the crowd."

I let her think about that for a moment.

"Where else could you possibly go and find two thousand people and not find an unhappy face in the crowd?"

"Heaven," she said, and put down the wine and the salad and walked away, still smiling.

Heaven? Of course.

It is not straining to say that Boston is heaven—or at least Mecca—to these runners. They come back every year, in growing numbers, to test this course, to test this race, to test themselves.

The thing to remember is this: They are here because they want to be here.

Nobody makes them come to Boston.

Nobody forces them.

They are here because at the heart of it all is the fact that they wouldn't be any place else on the 19th of April, which is Patriots' Day, the day of the Boston Marathon.

Erich Segal, the author and longtime lover of the Marathon, gets pretty esthetic about the Boston Marathon.

Erich tells us: "In our ever-more-mechanized, programmed society, marathoners want to assert their independence and affirm their individuality . . . call it humanism, call it health, call it folly. Some are Lancelots, most are Don Quixotes. All are noble. Whatever it is, our ailing world could use a lot more of it."

Or it's like my buddy Tommy Leonard, the bartender who runs in the Boston Marathon, was saying: "Jeez, with all the trouble going on in Boston these days, we ought to have a Marathon a month. It's the day everybody loves everybody else. I think we should give 'em all a beer. Give 'em three beers!"

Erich Segal may write better than he runs and Tommy Leonard may tend bar better than he runs. Not important. They run, and they love it, and they are better for it. That's very important.

Maybe you're like me. Before I saw my first Boston Marathon I knew little about the race. Once a year—around the start of the baseball season—I'd pick up the paper and there'd be that picture of those runners jammed into that street for the start of the race— so many of them that you wondered how they could get so many nuts together at one time. To run, what? Twenty-five miles?

Twenty-six miles? Ridiculous. I couldn't imagine myself in that mob for all the tea in Boston Harbor.

But you know something.

That picture always made me smile.

I don't know why. I never knew what it was. I'd see them in their caps, with handkerchiefs on their heads, wearing sunglasses —jammed together like five o'clock traffic—and I'd smile.

They were . . . different.

The amazing thing is that nobody named "Jones" has ever won the Boston Marathon. Not in eighty years. You'd think they'd have four or five Joneses by now. They've had a Smith and a Brown and a Hill and an Anderson. There have been two Kelleys—Johnny The Elder and Johnny The Younger. But there was also a Yun Bok Suh, an Eino Oksanen, an Edouard Fabre and an Aurele Vandendriessche, which I'll tell you how to pronounce later on. That's part of the Boston Marathon, too—its appeal around the world.

I've played a little game since seeing my first Boston Marathon and maybe you can try it at your local tavern.

I guarantee it'll go like this:

"Who won the Boston Marathon in 1969?"

"How the hell do I know."

"Okay, what's the greatest footrace in America?"

"The Boston Marathon."

So it's really not who wins. It's the people in the race. Big people. Little people. White people. Red people. Black people. Yellow people. Men people. Women people. Boy people. Girl people. And dogs. It is a fact that each April, on the 19th day of the month, these people—doctors, lawyers, plumbers, carpenters, clerks, book-keepers, soldiers, cops, mill hands, steelworkers, bricklayers, bill collectors, hairdressers, milkmen, students, husbands, wives, lovers —even the unemployed and those who don't have lovers—gather on that village green in Hopkinton to begin The Great Adventure. They hope to go the full distance—26 miles 385 yards—and experience that sweet feeling of success, crossing the finish line in front of the Big Pru. Maybe it's three o'clock. Maybe it's four o'clock. Maybe it's six o'clock and everyone has gone home. But if the Boston Marathon is about anything at all, it's about finishing: to conquer one's self.

THE BOSTON
MARATHON

1
Why Boston?

BEFORE THE 1975 RACE the press bus was parked outside of Prudential Center waiting to go to Hopkinton, Massachusetts. I'd talked Ray Fitzgerald into coming along with us. There is no better columnist in Boston, and yet, like so many of us, he had never taken time to see the Marathon. He was always over at Fenway Park, watching another ball game.

We were sitting there waiting for all the guys to get on when somebody shouted: "Hey, look! There's Catfish Hunter."

James (Catfish) Hunter. The three-million-dollar man. He was crossing the street on his way to breakfast. The Yankees were in town to play the Red Sox that morning and Hunter was out getting an early bite to eat. He was with two other guys, presumably also Yankees, though you can't tell about the Yankees any more. But nobody was paying a dime's worth of attention to them. The kids were crowded around the Marathon competitors' buses and they were getting the treasured autographs of Richard Fritz, Fred Fletcher, Bruce Aldrich, Thomas Bleakley, John Walsh, Bill Zucker and Claude Fowler.

The popular theory about the Boston Marathon—the reason for its universal appeal—is that anybody can enter it but not everyone can play in the Super Bowl or the World Series or go one-on-one with Jo-Jo White or try to stop Yvon Cournoyer from breaking in on the left side. I suppose this much is true. You can run in the Boston Marathon, the greatest event of its kind, if you are willing to pay a price. This is also the beauty of this race: You have to pay a price to get in. It's not the three-buck entry fee either. You have to push yourself, punish yourself—even torture yourself—if you want to be ready for this test of 26 miles 385 yards. You must put in those practice miles— forty a week, fifty a week, sixty a week. You must get out there before dawn, after dusk, in the heat, in the cold, in the sunshine, in the snow—and run. The present rules state that all male competitors under forty must have completed another sanctioned marathon in three hours within the year. Female runners and old gaffers over forty must do it in three and a half hours.

But you can get in on a lark, too. You don't have to pay the three bucks, and you don't have to put in the endless miles. Just show up at Hopkinton and you can run. Nobody knows who's official and who's unofficial. You can fool Jock Semple, the crusty guardian of the Marathon, and you can put one past Will Cloney, the reformed sportswriter who directs this race, but you can't fool the old Marathon. It'll get you. Maybe it'll be at Natick. Maybe it'll be at Wellesley in full view of all those screaming coeds. Nobody ever wants to drop out at Wellesley. Maybe it'll be at Auburndale, just before the hills of Newton. But it'll get you and it will bring you down and give you a lesson in honesty that you will not soon forget.

Nobody runs free in the Boston Marathon. They all pay a price.

And so now you ask—why Boston? Why not the American National at Galveston, Texas? How about the Jersey Shore at Asbury Park, the Marathon of the Times in Los Angeles or The Mountain, which is contested over the hills from Boone to Grandfather Mountain in North Carolina? Why is The Boston the epitome of marathon running?

For one thing it's the oldest race in America. It has more tradition and history than all the others combined. You tell somebody you've run in the Boston Marathon and you can earn immediate respect, even if they don't understand what the Boston Marathon is all about.

A fear among some is that the officials may destroy the very essence of this race if they keep making the entrance requirements too strict. The romanticists say, "Let 'em all run. Two thousand? How about twenty-five thousand?" Wouldn't that be a kick.

The runners in Boston seem special. Maybe it's because they are all God's children. They seem to understand charity and they seem to understand discipline. How many times in the course of eighty years has one runner paused to aid another. That's charity. And who will ever know of all the discipline that they put into their lives in order to prepare themselves to run in this race, this arduous test of one's self.

Children of God? The following article, written for *The New York Times* by Richard J. Israel after his first encounter with the Boston Marathon, perhaps more than anything else, gives an insight into this unique sporting event. It comes from one who took part in it himself—a man like you and me. Mr. Israel is the director of the Hillel Foundations of Greater Boston and in 1973 he took up running after two of his friends died of heart attacks:

Hooray for me! I scaled Mount Everest, pitched a no-hitter in the World Series and killed the meanest bull in Madrid. That is what it felt like when I won the 1975 Boston Marathon in 4 hours 16 minutes.

Will Rodgers thinks he won the Marathon in 2 hours 9 minutes 55 seconds, but he is wrong. Or, to be more accurate, he was running a different race.

He was trying to finish the race first. I and the people who were running alongside me in our segment of that incredibly long and colorful human ribbon were just trying to finish, to run the 26 miles 385 yards from Hopkinton to downtown Boston and remain conscious.

The registered runners with authentic numbers have officially qualified for the race. They look upon us with condescension. They wish we weren't around to clutter up the field. But happily, they can't or haven't chosen to do much about us. As a result, the Boston Marathon is the only major sports event in which I, a 45-year-old non-athlete, can participate.

I don't see why we cause them problems. How could I have got in their way? I never even saw the front-runners. It was two minutes after the gun went off before our part of the line moved an inch.

Our part of the race had three phases. Phase One was the sociable part, an occasion to find out where the next man (or woman) was from. Have you ever run before? What instrument do you play for the Buffalo Philharmonic? What pace are you running at? I'm trying for eight-minute miles, too. Let's stay together. Say, I know someone else who works at Goldman Sachs. You with the "Just Married" sign, your bride running, too?

In Phase Two, competitiveness began to enter our race. Conversations stopped, and running became a more individual matter. What a delicious experience to find those tall, lean, intimidating runners in the gorgeous track suits falling back (and they even had numbers).

We were in Wellesley, near the halfway point, when Rodgers won the race. That fact did not cast a pall on anyone near me. We were delighted with his time and record, pleased to be running in a noteworthy Boston Marathon.

By Auburndale and the beginning of the Newton Hills, the mood changed again. It became very sober. By this time, we were in Phase Three, and running was no joking matter.

I live near Heartbreak Hill, and jog up and down it almost every morning. I never knew why people made so much of it. But a two-mile incline, when it must be ascended after an eighteen-mile run, is absolutely devastating.

I *HAD* to get as far as the point where my kids were waiting for me. I couldn't let them down. I had sworn not to try to push myself beyond my natural inclinations (foolishly not realizing that twenty-six miles is beyond anyone's natural inclinations), but if I could get at least as far as the kids, I could quit.

I made it, and they were appropriately proud of me. That's nice, but this hill goes up for another mile. I can't keep it up. It just doesn't make sense to kill myself just because I said that I wanted to run the Marathon.

I knew that once I stopped, I would never be able to get started again. My legs wouldn't work. I stopped running and broke into a walk. I began to get cold. I knew I couldn't walk much farther, certainly not the remaining six miles.

Then a runner numbered U-6 appeared behind me. The extent of his English was the single phrase, "I Japan," though that was a larger vocabulary than I have in Japanese. He was about 65.

He saw that I have given up, took me by the elbow, got me going again, and continued to run or walk with me, arm in arm, whenever I got stuck for the next five miles. He wouldn't let me drop out. I was goaded on by his Japanese grunts, my thought of his age and my realization that the efforts he spent on me cost him his time.

U-6 wasn't doing that well himself. Given the physical condition of any runner at that point in the race, it was an overwhelming act of generosity. Without U-6's gift, I would have missed a peak experience of my life. I could never have done it without him.

By this time, none of us was running a race. We were trying to help one another survive an ordeal. There was no loneliness among the long-distance runners.

The rest of the way to the finish line was almost anticlimactic. When U-6 saw I was going to make it, he went on, and I never saw him again.

The end was a mixed bag of encounters with lovely encouraging spectators, drunks kicking beer cans across the street and offering passing runners shots of whiskey, and a scruffy brass band that urged us along. It began to get cold again. I was numb. My legs felt like stumps. But I had done it, and that was very good—very, very good.

It was suddenly all worth it. I had won. I had refused to accept a bad back, the middle-age paunch of a sedentary rabbi, even my mortality, and had triumphed over them.

I had changed from a late-sleeping nonexerciser who couldn't run around the block to one who eagerly gets up at 5 A.M. for a quick ten-mile run. I had just succeeded at some of the hardest things I had ever attempted.

It was exhilarating.

(After the 1975 Boston Marathon, Rabbi Richard J. Israel learned from a computer printout that the runner who had helped him during the race (U-6) was Tomiji Yamamoto of Japan. He invited Yamamoto to be a guest at his traditional Passover seders. Rabbi Israel spent weeks looking for a Japanese translation of the Haggadah, the text recited at the seder. He also arranged for a Japanese translator. Unfortunately, Yamamoto did not arrive in Boston until a half-hour after the second and final seder.)

"Oh, well," said Rabbi Israel. "I just tremble when I think I ran those twenty-six miles on matzohs. I suppose it did get our ancestors through the desert, but they did not have to make the trip in four and a quarter hours."

2
"They Shall Rise From the Dust"

THE BOSTON MARATHON IS:
- The oldest footrace in the United States.
- The only international long-distance race in the United States.
- The only road race in the United States where the spectators outnumber the participants 100 to 1 (at least).

The Boston Marathon is also Peter Foley. Good old Pete. He didn't take up running until his forties and he was eighty-five when he ran the full Marathon course.

Pete was a little slow, you understand. It took him a little while to get started. Sometimes it took him a whole minute after everyone else left the starting line.

His friends didn't like waiting for him—they had business of their own out on that long road to Boston. So good old Pete—wily old Pete—decided to run his own Boston Marathon. He took off at 10 A.M. and he was two hours down the road by the time the rest of the field started. This enabled good old Pete—shrewd old Pete— to reach the most crowded areas just before the leaders. And, if he timed things correctly, good old Pete—slick old Pete—would amble across the finish line about five minutes ahead of the legitimate winner.

The Boston Marathon is also Jimmy (Cigars) Connors, a blithe spirit who claimed he chain-smoked one hundred cigars on the way to town.

The Boston Marathon is also Chuck Mellor, who freely admitted to a liking of the bottle, which caused great consternation among the prohibitionists of his day. "Why do you drink when you run?" they asked indignantly. "It keeps my insides warm," replied Mellor, "and it tastes good." Go argue with the man. He won the 1925 race and broke the three-year reign of the incomparable Clarence H. DeMar.

But, pray tell us, how did all of this get started? Was it Paul Revere who made it a fad to go galloping through the New England countryside?

It all started with our old Greek friend Pheidippides, back in 490 B.C. He was the gallant warrior who ran twenty-five miles from Marathon to Athens with news of a great military victory, then fell dead after delivering the glad tidings.

That's what history tells us, if you care to believe history. It is difficult enough to spell Pheidippides, much less believe what he did. But it is a nice story—certainly harmless—and who can check it out anyway? The microfilm file in the *Boston Globe* doesn't go back that far.

For centuries the Greeks tried to think of a way to commemorate Pheidippides' worthy effort and at the first Olympic Games, held in Athens in 1896, they decided they would recreate his run from Marathon to Athens (but no fair anyone dropping out and dying).

It was a big success. The race was won by one of the local boys, a Greek shepherd by the name of Spiridon Loues. Marathoning was here to stay.

The B.A.A. (Boston Atheltic Association) sent a large delegation to Athens and the officials were so impressed they decided they would run their own marathon back on New England soil.

But New York beat them to it.

A group of New Yorkers were likewise impressed with Loues' feat and so they held the first marathon in the United States that very autumn—in October 1896. It was a run from Stamford, Connecticut, to Columbus Circle in New York City, and the distance approximated twenty-five miles. The race was won by J. J. McDermott, a name that would become part of the lore and legend of the Boston Marathon.

B.A.A. officials had to make two decisions: When to have the race and from where to where? They decided on April 19, and that was a nice touch, since it would commemorate Paul Revere's ride back in 1775. And they decided the race would begin at Metcalfe's Mill in Ashland and finish—in conjunction with a track meet—at Irvington Street Oval in Boston. Yes, that'd be nice. Just about twenty-five miles, give or take a few country lanes.

It was precisely at 12:15 P.M. on April 19, 1897, that Tom Burke, the starter, scraped the toe of his boot across the narrow dirt road in front of Metcalfe's Mill ("That's the starting line, gents") and called the field to order. He read out the numbers. Fifteen men answered.

While it seems like a humble beginning, the scene at the Mill was quite exciting. A lot of the folks had taken the morning train up from Boston and the baggage car was packed with assorted bicycles. They would pedal their way back to town with the runners. Others would stay to see the start, then hop on the train and get back to Irvington Street for the finish. There was a big mob out there for only fifteen runners.

Surprisingly enough, the officials showed great respect for the race. They sensed the dangers facing the runners. They had a militiaman and an ambulance corpsman accompaying each runner, flanking them with their bicycles. These aides handed out lemons, water and handkerchiefs and ministered to the runners when they fell by the roadside, which many of them did.

The roads were coarse and dry and the runners and the cyclists stirred up so much dust that some of the runners had difficulty breathing. The whole thing looked like they were running in the Oklahoma Dust Bowl.

The runners were shod in heavy boots and they wore toreador pants. They were setting a style fifty years before their time.

The race officially began at 12:19 and you'd have thought they were in a hundred-yard dash instead of a gruelling twenty-five mile run into Boston as everyone bolted from the starting line. Soon they began slowing down.

The crowd at Ashland Railroad Station, a mile long, was good-natured as it formed a line to permit the athletes to pass. The sleepy old town rang with cheers of her lusty sons.

The houses all along the way were filled with people and many handkerchiefs and good wishes were wafted upon the runners on this beautiful April day.

The competitors were feeling it already and "they ran with faces set."

That means it was starting to hurt.

From the *Globe*:

After leaving South Framingham, cyclists dropped in line about the leaders as if the heavens had suddenly opened and rained wheels. Carriages, wagons, motorcycles and every conceivable form of conveyance was brought into line. By the time the last runners left the square, there was hardly any room to turn about.

Several young women from Wellesley College received the leaders there, and when they recognized the Harvard colors of Dick Grant, they cheered.

Ultimately, it was J. J. McDermott of New York who was the winner. He took the lead at Newton Lower Falls and never relinquished it. But he paid his price, as would every Boston Marathon runner after him. He was so tired that he stopped five times from Boston College to the finish line and lost ten pounds during the long struggle, falling from 124 to 114. At one time he had an attendant massage his legs.

And wouldn't you know it—J. J. was so intent on just slogging along that he ran smack into a funeral procession along Massachusetts Avenue and caused two of the electric cars to stall.

But somehow J. J. got his second wind when he reached the track meet that was taking place at Irvington Street Oval. He was required to make one tour of the track—a 220-yard jaunt—and it was estimated that he did it in about forty seconds, which was quite good for this weary, dust-covered competitor.

Everybody cheered except J. J. He said: "Never again. I doubt I shall ever again run in a marathon race."

While J. J. was done, the Boston Marathon was just beginning. It would struggle through two wars and a depression; it would survive 90-degree heat waves and bitter cold weather; it would live through the pangs of overpopulation (both from runners and hecklers) and, of late, struggle through the wrath of women and joggers.

And what are they running for? The winner gets a floral wreath, while trophies go to the first ten finishers. Medals are given to the next seventy-five finishers. A special trophy is awarded to the "team" whose first three athletes finish highest in the race. That, and a plate of beef stew, if your belly can take it.

The *Globe*—tenacious devils—even found out what Pheidippides said in Athens before expiring. He said: "Rejoice! We have conquered!"

We'll let Howard Cosell check that one out.

3
Marathon Madness

THE BEGINNING . . .

It was a warm summer morning, the middle of July, as Tom Brown remembers it, in the days when he was the postmaster at Hopkinton—a job he held with distinction for thirty years.

Tom is weighing packages and tearing off stamps and selling them to customers when all of a sudden he looks up and—

Four young men are taking off their clothes.

Right in the middle of the post office.

"Hey!" Brown cries out. "You can't do that in here."

The youngsters just look at him and smile. They continue to disrobe.

Before Tom can get around the counter at them, he sees what they are up to.

They are runners, students from Harvard, and even if it is summertime, even if it is the middle of July, even if it is broiling out there—they are going to run their own Boston Marathon.

From Hopkinton to the Pru—26 miles 385 yards—just like the regular runners do every April.

The youngsters carefully package up their clothes and hand them to Tom.

"We'd like to mail these to Boston, please."

You can call it Marathon Madness—and it can strike at anytime in this little New England community (population: 5,981).

Marathon Madness.

Don't tell this to Mrs. Frances McMannus. To her, it is all perfectly normal—all very sane. She's been in the middle of it since her grandfather and the B.A.A. started running this race back in the 1890s.

Mrs. McMannus lives on Hayden Rowe, the starting point of the Boston Marathon, and once a year, right from her front porch, she has a box seat for the world's greatest footrace. She loves it. She sits there and watches the crowds plow through her hedge, photographers shinny up her maple tree, helicopters hover over her yard and state troopers rev their motorcycles over her normally serene street.

She wouldn't have it any other way.

"The Marathon puts Hopkinton on the map at least one day a year," she smiles, paying little mind to the candy wrappers, beer cans and occasional sweat suits that are beginning to accumulate on her lawn.

On April 19—Patriots' Day—Hopkinton becomes Pasadena on New Year's Day, Louisville on the first Saturday in May and Indianapolis on Memorial Day. Don't forget the Mardi Gras in New Orleans, the Easter Parade on Fifth Avenue and New Year's Eve at Times Square.

"It's really a big day for us," says Mrs. McMannus. "Why, it's even bigger than the Fourth of July or the high school football game between Hopkinton and Ashland."

It is truly mind-bending what takes place in this town on the 19th day of April. For 364 days a year Hopkinton sits quietly in the gentle New England countryside—26 miles and 385 yards from downtown Boston. Back in the 1880s this was a bustling community. That's when the boot-making plants were in full flourish. But strikes, then fires, then more strikes closed down all the plants.

Brigham Young also grew up here. This is where he got his religion, before taking it out west. He was born in Vermont, but Hopkinton is where he got his education. No, he never ran in the Marathon.

How about today?

"We've got a distribution center for Caterpillar Tractors—that's

12

pretty big," says Tom Brown. "And there's a place on the other side of town that make fire trucks. And there are a few electronic plants."

And that's it—for 364 days a year.

On the 365th, the whole community comes alive. They start arriving the night before (which is a neat trick since there are no motels or hotels in Hopkinton) and begin setting up for the big race.

The crush starts in the morning. They start spilling in from all directions. They come in cars, buses, on bikes, motorcycles, taxicabs, trucks—even on roller skates. (Skateboards have yet to make their appearance in the Boston Marathon. How do you get a skateboard up Heartbreak Hill?)

The Brown family has been slightly more than instrumental in conducting this race. It was George V. Brown, Sr., who was part of the U.S. delegation to the Athens Olympics and who first saw the marathon and brought the event back to New England. He personally started the race from 1906 to 1937, when he died. Brown had three sons—Walter, who would sustain the race while building a fortune as owner of the Boston Garden, the Boston Celtics and the Boston Bruins; George, Jr., who took over the starting duties from his father and still does it to this day (with the same gun), and Tom, who oversees a lot of minor details, such as trying to build a corral before the 1975 race so that they would have a proper place for the prime runners. They got the fence set up and it was working nicely until the school band came marching down the street. Gone: one corral.

"It's almost impossible to get all the runners together in the proper place at the right time," said Tom, while sitting in his car on Hayden Rowe. (How odd it must have seemed to him to see this street so quiet, so empty, so peaceful.) "We could line them up pretty well years ago, but that's when we only had a couple of hundred starters. Now, with thousands . . . I wonder about it sometimes . . . but then I think to myself, 'The more the merrier.' Anyway, Jock Semple is the only one who ever gets mad."

The runners—and they are all sizes and shapes—begin gathering at the gymnasium of the Walter A. Brown school. That's the official check-in point. But the Town Hall is open and so is every other available school. You can't get enough toilet facilities on Marathon morning.

Now there are thousands of people milling about—more than 2,000 runners and twice as many spectators.

Somehow everything is rather orderly.

In all the years they've been starting the race in Hopkinton, there has never been a single civil disturbance. Not a single arrest. Not a single fight.

It is organized confusion. There are no meetings about how to handle the mobs. The city workers know where they must set up the ropes, the Police Department knows where it must patrol—even the Fire Department knows where to set out its hoses.

"It's just not Hopkinton—but all along the route," says Brown. "It is really an amazing thing. Nobody tells those towns what to do. They just do it."

You might liken Hopkinton to the Augusta National Golf Course during Masters week. The conduct of the gallery there is also impeccable. Nobody dares throw so much as a hot dog wrapper on the ground for fear of reprisal in the way of an icy stare from a patron of the game.

Hopkinton isn't as clean as the Augusta National, but neither is it as dirty as some would believe—or as some would portray in the press. "Actually, we get it all cleaned up in a couple of hours," says Brown. "The runners really don't do much damage—not even to the bushes, as a lot of people believe."

The closest Hopkinton ever came to any trouble was the year one of the local condominiums opened its facilities to the "bandits" —those who run unofficially. They offered them shelter and a van on which they could put their gear to be taken to Boston. The only one who got upset was Jock Semple.

In days past—before the high school gym was available for the check-in and attendant physicals—the runners gathered at the Tebeau Farm, which became known as the Marathon Inn. The B.A.A. paid fifty bucks to rent the place. The furniture was moved out so that the bare rooms would be ready for the crush of runners. Then, as now, they would sit around going through their last-minute rituals: rubbing themselves with various unguents, swallowing vitamin pills and standing on line—such a long line—to use the toilet facilities.

Any year you will find a cross section of the world lining up on tree-shaded Hayden Rowe in Hopkinton. You might find Takayuki Nakoa, a twenty-year-old student from Chukyo University, Japan.

He stands just five feet tall and weighs but 106 pounds. He runs with elbow-length white gloves, which would be suitable for the Boston Pops, if he can make it to town in time.

Or you might find Clovis Bourdelais, who is sixty-nine, just standing off to the side, watching the runners get ready. He's got a gleam of envy in his eye. Clovis Bourdelais no longer runs in the Boston Marathon. His feet hurt.

Then there is Geoffrey M. Watt, the Australian optometrist, who has a Schweppes-like beard, and Sub-Lieutenant Robert Pape of the Royal British Navy. And if you look carefully, there are a few Americans in the bunch, such as Scott Downs Hamilton, Jr., a tall, good-looking architect from Little Rock, Arkansas. He took up mountain climbing as a Fulbright scholar at Oxford, and in 1957, he was the only undamaged survivor of a Himalayan adventure that killed two of his companions. He now prefers horizontal surfaces for his sport.

There's O. Gardner Spooner, a retired milkman from New Bedford, Massachusetts. He was the Marathon's rookie-of-the-year in 1939 at the elegant age of fifty-one.

They are all here—from Miko AlaLeppllampi to Constantine Kotteakas to Courtney C. Spingmeyer—and soon they will be off and running for Boston.

This is an innocent-looking street, this starting point for the greatest of all marathon races. They line up in front of No. 17 Hayden Rowe and also in front of that white house with the simple sign—1843—on the door.

Down a ways there is another sign: "Speed Limit 25." Nobody pays much attention to that one.

Now it is almost time, and if you are wondering how it goes at the starting line—when you've got more than two thousand foot racers lined up and ready to run—it goes something like this:

The official timer is Ellery Koch and when it is five minutes to go, he tells George Brown, the starter.

Brown informs everyone: "Five minutes to go!"

So far, so good.

It is amazing how still they all stand. Nobody is pressing forward, nobody is edging out.

When it's a minute to go, Koch gives the information to Brown, who is now on a stepladder with his blank .22 caliber pistol, and he informs the runners: "One minute to go!"

Then it is 30 seconds.

Then 25 . . .

Then 20 . . .

Finally—5, 4, 3, 2, 1—and precisely at noon, by Ellery Koch's watch, the gun goes off.

The pack moves like a giant glacier. Only the ones in the first few rows are able to start running. The others are jumping up and down, jiggling nervously, anxiously.

Now they are moving down the street, slowly, very slowly, like molasses from a bottle.

It is this moment for which they wait an entire year. In this moment all of them are heroes. In this moment there are no lonely faces in the crowd. They see and they taste and they smell the joy of man facing a challenge. They are now brothers in arms against a natural enemy.

A kid sitting up on a light pole yells: "Last one home is a rotten egg!"

. . . THE END

Gone are the happy faces of Hopkinton—the joy, the anxiety, the anticipation. In Boston, at the finish, the basement of the Prudential Building looks like a hospital ward during the Crimean War.

They are sprawled out everywhere—on cots, mats, blankets, some of them on stretchers, a few in wheelchairs and a lot of them just flat out on the concrete floor of the garage. They can go no farther. This is the end of the Boston Marathon, this bizarre, yet beautiful, race.

These men and these women have no more to give. They have nothing left to prove. They have concluded their mission. Some of them are on their stomachs. Some are looking up at the ceiling with empty expressions on their faces.

"I cried twice out there," says Walt Gantz, a twenty-nine-year-old student from Michigan State University. "It was beautiful. The people all along the way, standing there, cheering, yelling to you. I couldn't help myself. I cried twice."

Gantz has known the frustration of the Boston Marathon. Twice he suffered the ignominy of walking in. This time he wore a Mickey Mouse shirt to gain attention and the fans were yelling: "Hey, get going—Minnie is waiting for you!"

"They weren't trying to humiliate me," said Gantz. "They were trying to spur me. They wanted me to finish. They were offering me beer and everything else."

The young man broke into a smile.

"It was pretty tempting."

Now he sat up on his cot. "But this time . . . this time I was a runner. I love to run. I can't help myself. I just love it. I suppose I'm a cliché to the rest of the world but I'm so happy now I can't believe it."

Out in the hallway a small woman stands by herself. Sylvia Weiner is barely 100 pounds, just under five feet. She is forty-four years old. She has sad, black eyes and dark, curly hair. She is from Montreal, the mother of three children and she has just completed her second Boston Marathon.

"I made a terrible mistake last year" she says shyly. "I did not drink anything during the race—not a drop. I was too embarrassed to take anything from the people along the way."

Mrs. Weiner had finished in 3 hours 47 minutes and 31 seconds. The time, in itself, is unimportant. The feat of running 26 miles and 385 yards is everything.

Mrs. Weiner is a Polish refugee; she spent most of World War II in German concentration camps.

"That's what drove me on," she said. "I kept thinking of how hard my life used to be, how very close to death I was on many occasions. That's what kept me going.

"It may be a foolish thing to run but I have always wanted to survive. I always had the will for it. Now I have a victory—a victory for me."

Another woman, Nina Kuscsik, who led all the women runners home in 1972, is standing against a wall. She is being interviewed by several reporters.

An attractive woman, a registered nurse, she is telling them how her divorce spurred her into running.

"I went through a terrible ordeal," she says. "The divorce knocked me for a loop. All of a sudden, you are left with complete care of the children [she has three] and you have no medical insurance and no credit.

"I had to get myself straightened out. I had to do something to help my self-image . . . to know that I was still important."

She took up running—and beat her ex-husband by eleven minutes.

17

he said. "When he came to he had me carry him over to a desk where he picked up an entry blank for another marathon in New York!"

The final job, and perhaps the most time-consuming, is figuring out the order of finish. This is the duty of Dick Flynn of West Roxbury, Massachusetts. He supervises the hand-lettering of names, times and places of finish for each of the runners who comes in at 3 hours 30 minutes. The certificates are provided by Prudential —which is a nice policy.

4

The Route:
Trail of Terror

These high wild hills
and rough uneven ways
draw out our miles
and make them wearisome . . .

—SHAKESPEARE, from *Richard II*

TO RUN IN THE BOSTON MARATHON, here's all you do: Start at
Hayden Rowe and Town Green in Hopkinton, at noon, turn right
at the corner, onto route 135. Take route 135 to Ashland, Framingham, Natick and Wellesley, where route 16 joins 135. Continue
through Newton Lower Falls to Comonwealth Avenue, turn right
on Commonwealth (no ladies, you don't have to put your hand
out) and now you are on route 30. Take this through the Newtons,
Chestnut Hill Avenue, leaving the Reservoir on the right, to Cleveland Circle, Beacon Street to Kenmore Square, Commonwealth
Avenue again, right into Hereford Street and finish in front of the
Prudential Center Plaza.

Notice anything missing?

Sure.

The Wall. The Wall of Pain.

They never tell you about that when you send in your three bucks to enter.

That's because you can't see it.

But, boy, can you feel it.

Some runners live in fear of it. Some live in terror of it. Some don't even want to talk about it. Their eyes avoid you at the mere mention of it. They'll change the topic to something more comfortable: "Do you think Bobby Orr is worth three million dollars?"

But they know it's out there and that it must be conquered. They know they must break through this invisible barrier—this physical and psychological wall of pain—if they are to be successful in the Boston Marathon.

Some succeed, some fail. But they all feel the weight of the wall on their tiring bodies. The eternal challenge of any marathoner— old or young, fast or slow, male or female—is to finish. To accomplish this, every runner must increase his own capacity for pain.

In the Marathon this comes—almost without exception—at the twenty-mile mark. That's where the body and the mind begin to rebel. As the great Australian coach Percy Cerutty says, "Anyone can run twenty miles but few can run a marathon."

It is at the twenty-mile mark that the electrolytes—the life-giving salts, potassium and magnesium—begin to abandon the body. The body begins to dehydrate. It undergoes a traumatic chemical change and no amount of training can avoid this pitfall.

Each runner is affected differently. Some suffer from fatigue. Some grow dizzy. Some experience blurred vision and even depression.

But they all feel it.

What sets the Boston Marathon apart from all other marathons —and makes this such a great challenge—is that "The Wall" is encountered at the most insidious time of all, just as the runners hit the fabled hills of Newton.

The hills themselves are not that demanding. They are not that steep. Even the celebrated Heartbreak Hill, the third and final of these plateaus, rises only ninety feet. But its positioning, like the other two hills, is what makes it so murderous and explains why it extracts such a heavy toll.

The runners will tell you that Yonkers is tougher. Or any run through the desert. But nowhere is such a concentrated stress put on the runners as when they hit those hills of Newton.

The runners prepare for it in their own special ways. Tom Ward, the casket-maker from Aurora, Indiana, was seen pinning gumdrops on his shirt before the start in Hopkinton.

"You never know when you'll need energy out there," he said. "My trouble is I start hallucinating when I get to Heartbreak Hill. I always think of pancakes and syrup, and I don't even like pancakes and syrup."

Bob Keiss carries a radio with him and hopes he can find some upbeat music—a fast-paced commercial like the "Pepsi Generation"—when he's going into the hills.

As all marathon routes are supposed to measure, the route of the Boston Marathon measures 26 miles 385 yards (though some experts think it is a trifle longer). In any case, it took them a long time to settle on the accepted distance.

In the first run from Metcalfe's Mill, the course measured 24½ miles, and since that was close enough to the Olympic distance of 25 miles, nobody did anything about it. Why quibble over a few hundred yards when there were miles and miles to be run?

It was at the Olympic Games in London, in 1908, that the official marathon distance of 26 miles 385 yards was established. There was some sickness in the royal family and they were unable to attend the race. So the officials brought the start to them at Windsor Castle. This extended the race by a mile and 385 yards. And that's been the magic figure down through the years. It took time for the Boston folks to adjust their course properly. They thought they had it ironed out in 1924, but a close measurement showed them to be still 176 yards short. Road revisions down through the years, especially in the early 1950s, chipped away other portions of the course, forcing the starting line back to where it now rests, at the village green in Hopkinton. The final revision was made in 1965 when the finish line was moved from Exeter Street in front of the Lenox Hotel—which was also the site of the old B.A.A. building—to the new Prudential Center.

No matter how much they've altered the course, the runners still have to go through those hills at Newton at the worst possible time in the race.

Let me tell you about Tommy Leonard and the Boston course. He is part of this story, even if he doesn't think so. Tommy is forty-three. I think of him as a kid because, at heart, that's exactly what he is. In his heart he is still running the streets of Boston in his sneakers. He is still getting up early so he doesn't miss out on any of the street games, and he stays out late at night because there's always one more game to play, one more argument to be won: "Whatta ya mean Joe Gordon? Bobby Doerr can play rings around him any day." Tommy Leonard is single and he's a bartender and he's a kid. He is a beautiful person.

I met him through Joe Concannon at the *Globe*. We drove over to the Eliot Lounge one night and right away I knew what Joe meant about Tommy. Outside the bar was a hand-painted sign: "Good Luck Will Rodgers Olympic Trials." Tommy Leonard loves running, and runners. Before the 1976 race he conned one of the breweries into giving him a couple of hundred bucks so he could rent the flags of all the countries running in the race. He hung them from the ceiling of the Eliot Lounge. "Looks like the United Nations, don't you think?" grinned Tommy. He has one whole wall of the bar filled with pictures of the runners—all kinds of runners.

The two things Tommy Leonard loves most in life is running and Budweiser—sometimes not exactly in that order. When I told him I'd like to interview him, he thought it was a put-on. "Interview me? You gotta be kidding. I'll get Billy Rodgers in here for you and some of the other guys—the class runners. I'm just a plodder. You don't want to talk to me."

But that was precisely why I wanted to talk to him—because he *was* a plodder. We made a date for the following Sunday night at the bar and Tommy showed up, bombed.

He was true to his word, though. He did have all the runners there—including Rodgers, who set the Boston Marathon record with his sensational run in 1975. Tommy tried to talk into the tape recorder. "But thish thing jesh isn't working out," he stammered. We agreed to try it again—in the morning next time—and would he drive out to Hopkinton with me and go over the course? "Yesh, sure, anything you say, Joe baby."

There he was—as he had promised—in the lobby of my hotel at nine o'clock the following Tuesday morning. So come along with us to Hopkinton, we're going to do the 26 miles 385 yards in my rented Mustang. Bring on those hills of Newton! Bring on that wall! We're going to smash through them all.

"Jeez, I feel creepy," said Tommy, looking around at the green in Hopkinton.

"What do you mean?"

"The people . . . where are the people? It's spooky around here. I don't like it. I'm used to seeing people in Hopkinton. Let's get going, okay."

(HAYDEN ROWE AND TOWN GREEN)

"You're about three-quarters of the way back and it's one big shuffle coming out of this street. You let out a yell—like a big Indian yell: 'Yahoooooo!' All the people are screaming and yelling. I'm so far back I don't even know when the race is starting. The band is playing—God, I'd like to shake hands with every person on the way. They're so nice, so friendly. They just go overboard for us.

"How did I get started running? I guess it was at the orphanage. My folks were too sick to take care of me and I guess I was about seven at the time—I know I'd never been separated from them before. At least I'd never been out of Westfield, Massachusetts. I didn't want to leave them, but my father, he took me to the orphanage. They talked me into going into the dining room to have pancakes. Jeez, I didn't want any pancakes. I was crying and the tears were going right on my plate. Finally, they said to go into the playroom, and now I knew my father was gone. I just had a shopping bag with some clothes in it but I jumped out the window, the back window, when nobody was looking. I remember . . . jeez, it's been so long . . . I landed in the snow right up to my neck. I got out and started to the highway. I thought I was headed for Springfield, but I was headed for Pittsfield, the wrong way to go. I was picked up by a family and they brought me to the police station. And right back to the orphanage I went.

"I was always running away. I ran away a couple of times. The day Franklin D. Roosevelt died. I didn't have much money, I was always barefooted—I had short pants and no shoes but I took off the day Roosevelt died. I got as far as West Springfield. I guess this was 1945. April, I think. I got to the four-mile mark [laughter] and got hit by a thunderstorm. I was standing outside this K of C hall when the people invited me in. They gave me some water and a lady gave me a quarter so I could take the bus to where my aunt and uncle lived. They were looking for me at the orphanage—my father had died in the meantime and I'd seen my aunt and uncle around Christmastime, so I thought maybe I could live with them.

25

Again the police came and I spent a few hours in the Springfield jail. I went back to the orphanage and the next day they made me mow the lawn. It must have been six inches high and they gave me a rusty mower, like it was punishment."

(ASHLAND)

"Around thirteen, I guess, I lived in a lot of foster homes. I lived with this elderly lady who took care of me and I got close to the family next door. I was always baby-sitting for them. I came home from a football game one day and this lady I lived with, she was on the floor with a heart attack. They took her to the hospital and so I moved in with the people next door. Hey, there's Romeo's super-market on the right! Good old Romeo. I like to look at things but I'd rather look at the people. You see such happiness in their faces.

"I guess I really started running at Westfield High. I wasn't any good—look at the sign on the lamppost: 'Five Miles.' Jeez, we've gone five miles already! This year—I quit after seventeen miles, you know. I never quit before. The first time. The people were so great with all their water and their hoses. God bless them. I told Joe Concannon we ought to have a marathon a month. My first race in school was a mile and all I got was a mouthful of cinders. I was next to last. But I was kind of happy-go-lucky, and I remember in my senior year when we had the West Massachusetts Mile. We had our prom the night before and I showed up at the meet with my tuxedo pants and my suspenders. I was still whacked out a little bit. It was hot, like ninety degrees, and I came in fourth."

(FRAMINGHAM)

"I started running in the Marine Corps. It was during the Korean War. I volunteered but they wouldn't send me overseas because I was an orphan. I was stationed at the Portsmouth, New Hampshire prison. I was a guard at the prison. The C.O. was an ex-runner from Harvard and when he found out I was a runner, he gave me time off to run. I'd be running up and down the beaches but I guess he wanted it to be more official, more formal. He said, 'From now on, you will have two days off, you will have an escort, you will run on schedule'—he really ate it up.

"Hey there's the Happy Swallow! I'm always glad to see the first bar. I'm always tempted to go in for a drink. [Laughter.] But naw, I never took running seriously. In the old days, I never trained. Maybe I'd start getting serious around February fifteen but I just ran

26

for the fun of it. Jeez, I've gotta get my weight down. If I didn't run, I'd probably be dead now from the amount of beer I drink. I drink an awful lot of beer, Joe. I like beer.

"When I run, it flushes everything out. The poison. It keeps it down. It's like an internal shower. But the main thing is the friendships. I'd have never met Billy Rodgers if I didn't run. What a tremendous person. What a tremendous example for youth. There's no hassle about him. He's dedicating his whole life to emotionally disturbed children. You hear about these professional athletes and their negotiations and their contracts and you get fed up. If I was a kid I'd like to look up to somebody like Billy Rodgers. In Europe and Asia, why, he's a god. I've heard it myself. I was in Puerto Rico. I heard them down there talk about Billy. They didn't talk about the Bruins or the Celtics—they talked about Billy Rodgers. He's more than a runner—he's an artist. He runs on his toes. I don't know how he does it, but that's what he does."

(NATICK)

"Look at the lake over there. Sometimes I feel like going fishing in there. Sometimes I feel like jumping in. [Laughter.] I don't know if I can talk for twenty-six miles. If I just had a couple of Buds. The thing about running—and it's medically proven—is that it's the best form of exercise. Running and swimming. They're on a par. But you can't always get to a swimming pool and sometimes it's winter. Your heart and your lungs is what keeps you alive. You don't have to press bells—running is what helps your heart and your lungs.

"I don't believe I dropped out this year. I was talking to Billy Rodgers the night before the race—I guess I'm just a stubborn Irishman. He told me not to run. I guess I came out here and I was defensive right from the start. Hell, I was wobbling at the five-mile mark. Aw, Christ, it was bad. You can't run that way. But I wanted to try it. I guess I've got a little of the hambone in me—this is the longest stage in the world and I'm one of the performers. I like show biz. I'd be lying if I said I didn't. I like to hear the applause. You see that church over there? I always bless myself whenever I pass *any kind* of church. I guess I got that from parochial school. But I really don't run for the applause. I'm a nobody. I'm a plodder. I guess I've developed an acute appreciation of the esthetics in life. I'll look at a sundown and flip out. The best things in life are free.

27

Smelling the fresh air. Hearing the birds sing. I can be running through the woods and just listening to the wind whistling through the trees and a babbling brook and I'm happy.

"It's good for working things out in your head, too. I've gone out for a ten-mile run with a lot of things on my mind. I work things out. Sometimes I procrastinate, then I get out there and run and I feel better. It's a little tough at the start but when you get back and jump into that shower—running is the best thing for a hangover. You just wash it all out of you."

(WELLESLEY)

"I could go over this course blindfolded. The girls—I love 'em when they come out at Wellesley. All good-looking chicks, too. I try to make dates with them—'Meet you at the Eliot Lounge.' None of them ever showed up. [Laughter.] I guess you can say I'm O-for-twenty-one years. But I've done pretty well after the race. I don't have to depend on Wellesley.

"You start seeing them . . . right . . . about . . . now! Oh, wow—five hundred females screaming and yelling! I love to hear them laugh. 'Hey, girls! You look great! I love you!' I don't care who it is—who you are—it gets to you. I need the people. I need them to get me in. I don't train very hard, you know. I'm just a plodder. A mediocre plodder."

(NEWTON LOWER FALLS)

"I'm starting to get flaky now. It's mind-blowing what you go through out there. I'm thinking of the hills now and that spooks me a little. But it doesn't make much difference. I'm so flaky I don't know if I'm going up or down the hills. Strictly tapioca. God, I wish I was running now. I wish they had the marathon today instead of April nineteenth. I've got to requalify, you know. I had to qualify two years ago. I had to go down to New York, to the Westbury racetrack. You had to go around the track for a quarter of a mile, then go out on the golf course and do four six-mile loops."

(AUBURNDALE)

"Sometimes I'm seeing double. It's crazy. Everything gets hazy. You run along and you don't see a thing. Just the ground. I remember a little place called Mary's Café. It's not there any more. I used to go in there for a beer. They always looked forward to me coming by. I'd shake hands with all the people and they were great, really great. I wrote a letter one year and thanked them. Do you

28

know what? They put that letter up in the bar. Me, Tommy Leonard—I was a big man in Mary's."

(WALNUT STREET—NEWTONVILLE)

"Here they come—the hills! I'm a little spacy now. I just don't feel normal. It's not like drugs. I never took a pill in my life. It's just a buzz, like you get with too many Buds. I see the policemen now and I know a lot of the runners take them for granted. They do a helluva job on this day. So I try to thank as many of them as possible. 'Thank you, officer.' I try to smile, and they smile back. I mean, what's it cost?

"I remember once, this little old lady is standing on the curb and she's saying, 'Son, why don't you stop this foolishness and have some nice lemonade.' I looked at her and said, 'No, ma'm—thank you, ma'm, but no, thanks.' That's the way people are. I remember going to a Patriots' game. It was disgusting. These guys, all they wanted to do is start trouble. They were drinking and they got foul-mouthed and there's all these kids sitting around them listening to this language. I don't know why people are so hell-bent on destroying things."

(HEARTBREAK HILL)

"Sometimes I think I should walk up this hill but, jeez, did you ever see me walk. If I'm walking, little old ladies go by me. I'm probably the slowest walker in the world. So I always run up Heartbreak Hill, no matter how much it hurts. I remember the first time I saw a girl go by me. I wanted to take off my shoes and throw them in the river. Now . . . now I love them. God bless them all. I think some day girls are going to make better marathoners than guys. Honest. They can take more pain. They have babies and they have periods and they can put up with a lot more than we can. I'm not looking for—hey, we went right by Woodland where I dropped out this year. Do you believe that? It must be a mental block. I can't believe we went right by it. It was just before the fire station. My sister was there with some friends and she says, 'Tom, I've got a bucket of Bud in the van.' That's all I had to hear. I stopped. Just like that. I stopped. I just walked off. Can you imagine that? I gotta start getting serious."

(COMMONWEALTH AVENUE)

"They had a place over there, across the street, called The Tam. I used to stop in there, too. It was a famous pit stop. [Laughter.] One

29

year they had a whole band waiting for the runners. I only wish all Boston would turn out like that. I mean the bar owners. Just think, if every bar gave one free beer to every runner—Christ, there's more than two thousand bars in Boston. Some guys travel more than three thousand miles to get in this race. Roll out the red carpet for them. When I went into The Tam one year they had a bottle of champagne for me. We went chug-a-lugging and got right back on the track again."

(KENMORE SQUARE)

"You look for the Citgo sign—there it is! I love you, Citgo sign! I love you! It gets bigger and bigger, and then you know you're getting closer and closer. It's a big struggle for me now. They're all shouting, 'You're home! You're home!' But they've got that damned little hill by the overpass. I think they put that one in just for me. I have to work to get up there."

(THE PRU)

"Wow, they're all screaming now. Both sides of the street, all packed. You've got to run through single file. You try to slap their hands—I think that's important. I don't care who you are, or where you're from, they all know you. It must make a guy feel good to hear this crowd when he's from a place like Silver Lake, Idaho. I didn't think I could talk this much. I hope I had something to say."

5
Boston:
An Olympic Jinx

IT MAY BE SAID—and with considerable merit—that the greatest marathon is the Olympic Marathon. It is run every four years and draws only the world's class runners.

And yet, no Olympic champion has even won in Boston. Seven have tried, seven have failed.

Before examining this strange circumstance, let's look at marathoning at an Olympic level—since that's where it all started at the Olympic Games in Athens in 1896.

We mentioned earlier that it was Pheidippides, the old Greek warrior, who got all of this long-distance running started by racing from Marathon to Athens with word of a great Grecian victory—and then falling over dead. This is the version that is accepted in the western world. It seems you can get as many versions as you want merely by the number of history books you care to read.

One historian maintains that Pheidippides could not have run the 25-mile distance from Marathon to Athens because he had just completed a round-trip run to Sparta, a distance of 150 miles, in an attempt to enlist the aid of the Spartans in the fight against the Persians.

Anyway, the people in Greece knew that something special had happened back there in 490 B.C. and so they dreamed up the idea of a marathon run when the modern Olympic Games were inaugurated. (The Games, in fact, almost never got off the ground. The Greek government didn't have enough money to finance them and only a last-minute gift of one million drachmas from a Greek merchant made them a reality.)

Ill feeling would arise out of the first Games.

The Americans were winning almost everything in sight and the Greek newspapers were blasting away at the "professionalism in America." On the final day the Marathon was to be held and it was to be the highlight of the Games. The race began on the Plains of Marathon, at the precise point where the seven thousand Greek defenders had repulsed the twenty thousand Persian invaders. At each kilometer, couriers on horseback would gallop ahead of the field to carry news of how the race was progressing into the Olympic stadium.

As the fans in the Olympic stadium waited for the runners, they saw the riders gallop into the stadium and rush to the royal box, where Prince Constantine and Prince George of Greece were sitting. There, the couriers whispered the news to the monarch. The spectators knew from the royal reaction that things were not going well for the home side.

As the time approached for the first runners to arrive at the stadium, another courier sped into the stadium and this time he appeared excited. He gave his message to the two monarchs and then a loud roar began spreading throughout the stadium. Word had been received that a Greek runner—name not yet known—was nearing the stadium and nobody was in front of him.

Minutes went by . . . and then Spiridon Loues, an unknown shepherd, came jogging into the stadium. He seemed exhausted, but he plodded around the track while the fans went into hysterics. Prince George and Prince Constantine leaped from their box to the track and formed an honor guard on either side of Loues—and the three men crossed the finish line together.

Now there was pandemonium in the stadium. Greeks were hugging and kissing one another, embracing in laughter and tears. The honor of the country had been saved.

And that was only the first of many bizarre moments that would mark the Olympic marathon.

In 1904 in St. Louis, Fred Lorz of the United States was about to receive a gold medal from Alice Roosevelt, the daughter of President Theodore Roosevelt, for winning the marathon when irate officials went running to the victory stand crying "fraud." It seemed that Lorz had suffered from leg cramps at the nine-mile mark and hopped into a car and traveled the next thirteen miles in the back seat. Then, nearing the finish line, he jumped out at a blind curve and ran into the stadium pretending he was the victor. Lorz tried to explain it was only a joke, but the Olympics, even then, were no joking matter to the nations of the world.

Four years later the 1908 Olympics in London produced the most dramatic marathon ever run—in any part of the world. There is clear proof of exactly what happened since this was the first time the Games were filmed.

Dorando Pietri of Italy was first into the stadium. He was more than a quarter of a mile ahead of America's Johnny Hayes.

But then everything went wrong for poor Pietri.

He turned the wrong way and began running in the opposite direction to the finish line. He was redirected to the right path but he was totally exhausted, utterly spent and fell four times.

Somehow, he got up all four times.

The officials, fearing for his life, all but carried him over the finish line. Then Johnny Hayes entered the stadium, and while Pietri lay unconscious on the grass, Hayes was declared the winner.

He was America's last marathon winner until Frank Shorter won at Munich in 1972.

Apparently it is one thing to run in Athens, London, Munich—or any other of the Olympic sites—and quite another to run in Boston.

Tom Hicks, the 1904 Olympic champion from the United States, ran four Bostons but the best he could do was second place in 1904.

Hayes himself tried it three times but finished fifth, third and second.

Hannes Kolehmainen, the 1920 winner from Finland, had tried Boston in 1917 and wound up fourth.

Albin Stenroos, another of the great Finnish runners, won the Olympic gold medal in 1924 but ran second at Boston in 1926.

Delfo Cabera, the Argentine Olympic champion of 1948, tried Boston in 1954 and finished sixth.

Abebe Bikila, the only man ever to win two Olympic Marathons (1960 and 1964), set a record pace in Boston in 1963 but wound up getting cramps and finished fifth.

Mamo Wolde, Bikila's Ethiopian teammate and winner of the gold medal in 1968, finished no better than twelfth in the 1963 Boston Marathon.

Seven tried, seven failed. And Shorter—the U.S. champion of 1972—has never even tried Boston. Maybe he knows something.

6
Jerry Nason Recalls the Marathon— and Tarzan Brown

ACTUALLY, THIS BOOK should have been written by Jerry Nason. Why he didn't do it, I'll never know.

Jerry Nason happens to know more about the Boston Marathon than any man in the world. He saw his first Boston Marathon at the age of five days and you've got to admit that's a pretty early age to be following Boston Marathons.

The story goes like this: Jerry was born on April 14, 1909, in the old frame hospital in Newton, which was located on the course of the Boston Marathon. Five days later—on Patriots' Day, April 19— a nurse picked up young Jerry from his cradle and held him up to the window as the runners were trudging by. Jerry is pretty honest about it. He doesn't remember who was leading, though he thinks it was the Frenchman Henri Renaud: "My mother told me the story about being held up to the window and I'm not going to say anything against my mom."

Jerry covered his first Boston Marathon for the *Boston Globe* in 1933—and has done it every year since. He is retired now but comes back one day a year—on April 19—to lend his talented hand to this great race. Much of what is in this book was researched by Jerry Nason and it would not be fair—or game—to pretend otherwise. He is truly the Boswell of Boston.

Frankly, I was apprehensive about going to see him and talking about the book. What if he resented me, an outsider from Detroit coming into his territory and writing about the love of his life? What if he told me to bug off?

I mentioned this to the guys in the sports department of the *Boston Globe*.

"Naw," they said, "you've got Jerry all wrong. He'll be more than glad to see you. G'wan, call him up."

Still, it was with some apprehension that I dialed his telephone number and told him what I had in mind.

I didn't know this man and underestimated him badly. Jerry lives in Arlington with his lovely wife Jo, and he was saying, sure, sure, come on out. Did I know the way? Could he come into town to pick me up? How about lunch?

I took a taxi to his home in Arlington, a suburb of Boston, and we sat on the sun porch while Jerry's wife busied herself making lunch. We spoke for several hours. Jerry spoke from memory. He held a small black book in his hands and referred to it only once— when he gave me the list of Olympic marathon winners who had failed in Boston. His wife went to town to buy a couple of cartridges for my tape recorder.

"In the early days, each of the runners was accompanied by a rider on a bike, an attendant who carried a canteen of water and maybe some lemons and oranges for nourishment. We're talking about a long time ago. When we were kids in Newton—and I lived on the hills my whole life—we'd get up early on the day of the Marathon and ride our bicycles all the way out to Ashland, which is where they started the race at that time. We'd pick up some of the lower-case runners who had no attendants. It was a big deal to carry a knapsack for one of these runners. We had to wear a corresponding number to his, so we always had a ten-cent bet, a little pool, to see who'd get the farthest down the course. I once had a guy who made it all the way to Cleveland Circle, within three miles of the finish, and don't think I didn't tell everyone that *I* held the world's record. Do you believe this: I once got into a picture that hung in the *Boston Globe* for years and years. The first time I walked in there and saw it, I nearly fell over. I couldn't believe it was me. Here, coming down Commonwealth Avenue and in the lead, about to win his third or fourth Marathon, was Clarence H. DeMar, and right behind him was the official car containing all of the bigwigs of the race and right behind them—pedaling his heart out with a cap on his head and wearing a pair of knickerbockers—was none other than Jerry Nason.

"Remember, in those days runners were mostly blue-collar workers. They'd work up to sixty hours a week and they got poor salaries. By our standards of today, they didn't have much leisure time for training. It was a big deal if they put in forty or fifty miles a week. And they didn't start training until about January. Today, these guys are going at it year round.

"You've got to remember there were only three marathons in the country at that time—Boston, Yonkers, New York, and Washington, D.C.

"Years ago they didn't have macadam roads until you reached Boston. This race started out in the country and the roads were muddy; they were filled with rocks and they had mud ruts in them from the wintertime. That's why these fellows had to wear such heavy thick-soled shoes. You could hear them coming down the street. It sounded like wet fish being slapped on a table. It was a big handicap to them, but if they didn't have those heavy shoes, they'd be turning their ankles or bruising their feet so they couldn't run at all. A lot of them shouldn't even have been in the race. It's that way today, but more so then. They had people who were doing it on a bet or a dare. We had a lot of that. MIT or Harvard students would come into the race maybe as part of an initiation into a fraternity. You'd always have ten or twelve college students in the race and this was in a field of only a hundred runners or so. They never got very far down the road and they were really a mess.

"The real runners would come in here on freight trains—riding the rails from places like Philadelphia and New York and Buffalo and Detroit. Even Chicago. The big thing with us kids is that we got to keep the number we were wearing.

"It used to irk me when I'd see how the Boston papers would treat the race. It was the same thing every year. They'd say: 'Spring must be here, the saps are running.' This was an old standard in Boston and it bothered me because these guys weren't saps at all. I knew how tough it was out there and what these guys were going through. They were pretty rugged individuals to be running that distance, and under those conditions. One runner—Dave Komonen of Ontario—was a cobbler and he made his own shoes. Even then they knew they couldn't run in sneakers because of all the blisters they'd get. They'd have to wear strong shoes and they must have weighed a pound apiece.

"My first realization that we had something that was indeed unique and unusual was when I went over to London to cover the Olympic Games in 1948. It was my first experience as a writer in an international event. It was the first time I'd ever been exposed to people from all over the world. It didn't take me long to figure out just what our race really meant. I'd be introduced to somebody from Japan or Africa or the Netherlands and they'd say, 'Ah, the Boston Marathon.' It was true with all of them, the Orientals, the Europeans, the South Americans. They kept asking me questions about the Marathon until I came home and started thinking about it myself. I realized that Boston didn't know what it had. Here I was talking to people from all over the world and they never heard of the Boston Red Sox or the Celtics or the Bruins or even Harvard and Dartmouth. But they knew about the Boston Marathon and our city had never done a thing with it to promote the race. In fact, most of the people in the city—especially the writers—generally made a big laughing matter out of the whole affair.

"Now I was pretty serious about it. I have to admit that. And I like to think that I was somewhat responsible for changing this attitude. I got along with the writers on the other papers; I never thought of them as enemies. So whenever we got together I'd start preaching this point to them—telling them what a helluva thing we've got here. Dave Egan of the old *Record*—he was what you'd call a knocker. He used to have all kinds of fun with the Marathon. But I'd talk to him, try to explain what it was all about, and I did this with the others, like Huck Finegan, and writers like that. I didn't try to overwhelm them and in time they started coming around. Radio used to ignore the whole thing. Maybe they'd tell you who was leading at the halfway point and then the winner, and that was about all. Now they all make a major effort, radio, TV and the newspapers.

"For years and years, up until 1947, the Marathon was covered by the six Boston newspapers, and each newspaper had its own car on the course. Each paper had a writer in the car and maybe two photographers. There were two official cars, so that made eight in all. And I'm not even counting the wire services, the AP, UP and International News Service. They had their own cars, too, so that there were maybe ten or twelve cars out there surrounding the runners. We'd all be concentrating on the leaders and we'd be jockeying back and forth to get in position to get the best photos. Now you gotta picture this whole scene: These guys are trying to run a race and here are twelve cars jockeying all around them. We'd say, 'Hey, the *Record* car is up front on the right. Let's try to get ahead of them.' We kept cutting in and out and back and forth. It was like a race within a race. It was like Indianapolis in slow motion. We'd be yelling at the other cars, 'Get out of the way!' and they'd be yelling back at us. All the while, mind you, nobody is thinking of the poor runners, who were being caught up in the fumes from these cars and all but being asphyxiated.

"Now in 1946 we had Stylianos Kyriakides, the starving Greek, and he comes over here and he's emaciated. The Greeks are starving to death after the war and he wants the world to know about it. He thinks if he can win the Boston Marathon he can bring attention to the plight of his people and something will be done about it. He and old Johnny Kelley have this terrific battle all the way. Terrific. But nobody ever saw it. They were surrounded by these automobiles—and vaguely, in this blue haze of gas fumes, you could see two guys in white uniforms, running. How either one of them finished, I don't know. But they had a tremendous duel right down to Kenmore Square, a mile from the finish. The Greek, from somewhere in his gut, put on a little sprint and beat old John and won the race. It was a very dramatic story. Word of it went all over the world and the Greeks did get some help. I remember being up in a room in the old B.A.A.—this was when they finished in front of the Lenox Hotel—and I'm sitting there with Kyriakides and Kelley and I'm interviewing them. As the Greek is telling me about the poor little children with no eggs and no milk, old Johnny Kelley is sitting there and the tears are streaming down his face. He's bawling like a baby. Here he has just lost one of the greatest Marathon races ever run and he's blubbering all over the place. That's what this race can do to you.

"It was the next year that Walter Brown, who's dead now . . . he used to put on the races . . . he was the race director . . . Walter said, 'Look, this race is getting ridiculous with all those cars out there.' So the next year he eliminated all the autos and put everyone into one bus. Right away the times picked up noticeably. The runners didn't have the cars impeding them and they didn't have to suck up those fumes into their lungs. A good time was 2:30.

That was good for anyone. Pretty soon, when the Koreans started coming in and the Japanese, they were running under 2:20. Nowadays the runners will complain if there's one state trooper out there—one motorcycle dropping a little carbon monoxide on the course. They don't know what it was like when it was really suffocating out there.

"I can't let this moment go without talking about the most fabulous, the most fantastic man ever to run in the Boston Marathon. There was an Indian boy down on the Narragansett reservation in Rhode Island back in 1936. He was fatherless. He started running in '35 and I saw him in a twenty-mile race in Medford and couldn't believe my eyes. He had a shirt his mother had made for him, a running shirt, and it looked like those crazy quilts they made in the old days. She took a little bit of this material, a little bit of that material—anything she could find—and pieced it all together and that's how Tarzan Brown showed up to run.

"Now, Tarzan was different. You must understand that right away. He did his training in barrooms and he had some terrific brawls. He would have made a great welterweight. He was beautifully muscled and there wasn't an ounce of fat on him. He went out in the 1936 race—he didn't know anything about training or pace—and he ran his gut out. He had the biggest lead at Framingham of any man in history. He was five hundred yards ahead of everyone after just six miles. In fact, he got out so quickly that the press cars never saw him. We were following the other guys, thinking they were fighting for the lead. When we got to Framingham, the timer said 'What kept you guys?' We said, 'We're following the leaders.' He laughed: 'You're nuts. The leader went through here about two or three minutes ago.'

"Of course he meant the crazy Indian. That's what we used to call him—'Chief Crazy Horse.' My God, could he run. He was running like Zatopek pacing the Olympic marathon twenty-five years later. He held his lead until he broke every checkpoint record for twenty-one miles. He was going to break the overall records by a full ten minutes the way he was going. But then the pace started taking its toll on him. He got down to those last five miles and slowed to a jog. Old Johnny Kelley came on with a terrific rush from Wellesley, the halfway point, and he came up even with the Indian at the top of the hill at Boston College. I'll never forget it and I'm sure Johnny never will either. Just as Johnny was going by the Indian—in a friendly way, you understand—he patted the

Indian on the bottom of the ass, as if to say, 'Nice run, pal. Nice try, boy.' The Indian looked up and took off like a rabbit. It was like Johnny Kelley had put a pin up his ass. Johnny never caught him again. The Indian got so far in front that he stopped about two miles from home and began walking. He'd walk a little, jog a little and won comfortably. This was an Olympic tryout. It was an Olympic year and so Tarzan Brown won himself a place on the United States Olympic team. He still didn't know anything about running. I only wonder what would have happened if he had lived closer to Boston and had a coach—but he went over to Berlin and again paced the field. But Tarzan wasn't doing much training, except in the beer halls over there. In fact, as I remember it, he spent two nights in the clink before the race, because he got into a brawl with some of Hitler's Blackshirts. They had to spring him for the race and he led the Olympic marathon for thirteen miles and was still second for eighteen miles. As he told me later, he got a terrible pain in the pit of his stomach and he sprawled out on the side of the road. A man, a German spectator meaning well, started picking him up just as an official car came by. They shouted to Tarzan: 'Out! You're out of the race! You are disqualified!' Tarzan walked in the rest of the way and he was pretty angry about it because he hadn't asked the spectator for any help.

"Tarzan took a big ribbing about it when he got back home to Rhode Island and now he got madder than ever. And this is the most unbelievable part about this man because it was then that he pulled off one of the most remarkable feats in the history of athletics. Tarzan decided he was going to make these people eat their words and so he entered two marathon races, held on consecutive days, Saturday and Sunday, one in Yonkers, which was the New York championship, and the other in Manchester, New Hampshire, which was the New England championship. Tarzan won the first race in Yonkers and then hitchhiked—hitchhiked!— to Manchester and won that race even though he didn't get there until seven o'clock in the morning. Five days later he came down with a double hernia. For pure power—pure ability—raw talent and God-given strength, there was nobody like Tarzan Brown.

"I remember once, near the end of World War II, I heard that Tarzan was going to make a big comeback. He had won the Boston Marathon for a second time in 1939 and now I got word he was going to try for a third Boston crown. As I said, Tarzan lived on the Narragansett reservation in Rhode Island. His grandfather had been chief of the tribe, or what was left of them. Most of them had been wiped out in King Philip's war. So I got a camerman and we drove down to Rhode Island and there, right out in a clearing in the woods—you had to walk in along a cow path—there was Tarzan and his family. Some of the trees had been chopped down and he had built himself a tar-paper shack with shingles made out of the bark of trees. Now picture this: Tarzan Brown, his wife, their four kids, lived in this clearing in the woods. I must have written a million words about him but I had no idea his life was like this. They had a brook—a stream—running behind their house and Tarzan had scooped out a big basin with his hands so they could bathe. Here was this undisciplined man, this untrained man, this child of nature—oh, I can still see him running, that dark skin glistening in the sun, those rippling muscles, like a highly polished carving—here he was, in 1945, living as if the white man had never come to this country.

"I remember the day they were coming through Natick. Four of them in one bunch. All were looking good. Tarzan looked the best. All of a sudden, he took off and jumped over the fence and dove into the lake. As we went by, there was Tarzan, bobbing up and down, waving goodbye to us. He was so raw, so crude, so undisciplined . . . so beautiful.

By Jerry Nason

CHARLESTOWN, R.I., April 13—Three hundred yards up a side road, in the brush country which ranges the shores of Narragansett Bay, squats a tar-paper shack, and all around it the trees and brush have been cleared away—backbreaking toil.

Within this crude, but watertight abode of two rooms live a man, a woman and their four small children—four kids with black snapping eyes, raven hair and a proclivity for suddenly darting up a tree with the ability of squirrels.

The man and woman, having lost their home in nearby Westerly, and being unable to rent a more suitable home on their limited finances in this housing crisis, dragged odds and ends from a dump more than a mile away and, together, built this shelter for themselves and their children.

The man is Ellison Myers Brown, noted, in a not too distant day, for being the swiftest of all distance runners . . . a man who, today, is driven by necessity into attempting to recapture the speed and endurance which twice sent him careening into Boston a winner of the annual Marathon race.

"Look around at this place where I live," said Tarzan Brown. "See for yourself! You'll know why I've got to do the only thing left to do—win the Boston Marathon race in world record time."

You look around and you see the small shack, crouched in a slight depression about twenty-five yards from the road; you see the home two desperate parents built with their own hands; the barren, but immaculate interior, with its two beds, one wood-burning stove to warm and feed the occupants, the outhouse back in the grove, with its flapping blanket for a door, the swimming pool Tarzan has scooped out of a rushing brook that serves both as bathtub and recreation center.

Whether or not Tarzan can drive himself to the superb racing condition needed for the mission nobody knows, not even his devoted brown-skinned wife. Tarzan is a child of nature. He earned his nickname over at Alton as an Indian boy who, like his progeny today, would scale the highest tree and shinny out on the longest bough at the drop of a hat.

"If Ellison keeps his mind on it," said Mrs. Ethel Wilcox Brown, "he probably can win it. I don't like to boast, but I think when he is prepared for it, he is the best runner of all."

Tarzan, almost penniless, with no steady job, is a husband devoted to the soft-spoken woman who, by his side, shared the labor of building this unpretentious abode—a father in whose black eyes shines a deep love and pride for the four little Browns who dash wildly around him.

Tarzan is now thirty-two, a magnificent physical specimen—broad shoulders, deep chested, buffed down to narrow hips. His legs are the envy of his opponents.

"I've trained for two and one-half months," said Tarzan. "I weighed 168 when I started. I'm about 153. Maybe that's good. I'm older now. Maybe that's the right weight.

"Maybe I can win the Marathon, maybe I can't. But I'll tell you this much—if I'm up there at twenty miles nobody's gonna beat me."

Tarzan has no false illusions. He knows that fame flees swifter than his own legendary limbs. He knows that laurel wreaths won at Marathon racing are not edible. He knows that his cups and trophies are gone and that he is a poor man with few of life's necessities.

At various times a stonemason, woodchopper, handyman and tree surgeon, Brown depends on odd jobs to feed and clothe his family. A few hours here and there in a coal yard at nearby Westerly, a tree to be taken from somebody's front yard—anything to earn a dollar.

43

"Folks in Westerly," he said, and not bitterly, "will pay some tree expert $75, gladly, to remove a big tree. If Tarzan Brown does it, he can't get more'n $20.

"Lot of prejudice around here. I had to go to New London to get my last haircut. They tell me in Westerly: 'We don't cut your kind of hair here!' And I say, 'Why not? My hair's as good as yours.' But they don't cut my hair for me.

"Maybe you heard I get in trouble sometimes. Maybe I do. Somebody takes a poke at me and my trouble is, I poke them back."

That accounts for the homemade punching bag down by the brook.

If Tarzan can win the Marathon, his objective will be to gain a little financial backing.

"If I could just get myself a truck, I could make a good living around here," said Tarzan Brown.

The curious thing in talking to Jerry Nason is that he sat back in his chair most of the time, but leaned forward when he said: "I can't let this moment go without talking about the most fabulous, the most fantastic man ever to run in the Boston Marathon." Up until then, I'd been asking the questions and Jerry had been answering them. But his story about Tarzan Brown came out of the blue. I had no idea what he was going to say as he leaned forward on his knees so he'd be sure that his voice went directly into the microphone of the tape recorder. I didn't know what he was going to say and trying to hide my ignorance, I blurted out: "Good, I'm glad you're going to talk about him."

I thought he was going to tell me about old Johnny Kelley or Clarence H. DeMar. And then when he started talking about this young Indian boy, I thought for sure he was going to tell me the tale about Tom Longboat, the Penobscot from Ontario.

When he mentioned Tarzan Brown, I was stunned. I didn't even know Tarzan Brown was an Indian. In fact, all I knew about him was that when we were on the press bus the previous year, John Ahern of the *Boston Globe* looked out the window as we were passing Lake Cochituate in Natick and said, "Here's where old Tarzan Brown jumped into the water," and everybody laughed. I thought Tarzan Brown was some local yokel—I mean to have a name like Tarzan he must have been some kind of nut and somebody must have hung that moniker on him strictly as a gag. Like maybe he swung from chandelier to chandelier in the local pubs.

But it was clear, in only a matter of moments, the deep feeling

44

—the affection, the compassion, the admiration—that Jerry had for this Indian lad. I mentioned this to Johnny Kelley, in my visit to Kelley's home out on the Cape, and Kelley said: "Aw, that Nason . . . he's always talking about Tarzan Brown." Kelley's comment bothered me. It was one of envy and I wondered why old Johnny Kelley—a hero to all Boston, the one they all wait for and cheer every Patriots' Day—would be upset at the mere mention of this Indian's name.

After leaving Jerry's house, I did some more checking into Tarzan Brown's background and found—surprisingly—that he was a very well-spoken man for one who never got out of the seventh grade. I thought he only ran on his God-given ability but it turned out that he had acquired a sound sense of running.

"The Japs train better than we do," Brown told Jack Barry in another interview, ten years after Jerry Nason's visit to Rhode Island. "I say the Americans should go over to Europe or Japan two months before the Olympic dates in order to get used to the climate, the hills and the country. I think if I had had three more weeks in Berlin I could have won the 1936 Olympic marathon.

"The greatest miler of all time was Glenn Cunningham. He was a powerhouse. He had strength, legs, stamina. Way back there he was doing the mile in 4:04. I think in less than ten years guys will be running the mile in 3:50. And without doubt, the greatest marathon runner of all was Clarence H. DeMar."

He remembered to put the H. in his name.

No, Tarzan Brown didn't win another Boston Marathon. He never got to set that record he so eagerly sought. And, as nearly as anyone knew, he never got that truck to make a "good living around here."

(Epilogue)

WESTERLY, R.I., Aug. 24, 1975—Ellison M. (Tarzan) Brown, 61, who competed in the 1936 Olympics and twice won the Boston Marathon, was killed yesterday when he was run over by a car in the parking lot of a bar.

Police said Brown was struck by a car driven by Phillip Edwards, 26, of Middletown, Conn. Police said the incident occurred after Brown and Edwards had an argument.

7

The Bob & Jerry Show

IT WAS WITH GREAT JOY—and considerable astonishment—that Bob Keiss and Jerry Coyle informed me on the night before my first Boston Marathon that we would have to go out to dinner and stock up on as much spaghetti as our tummies could hold.

"Gotta pack in those carbohydrates," they said.

"Yeah," I replied, "gotta pack in those carbohydrates."

Of course, the only difference was that they would negotiate the 26-mile 385-yard distance on foot while I would cover it from a seat on the press bus.

We went to an old restaurant in the Italian section of Boston, near the tunnel, and I guess they thought they were good spaghetti-benders until they saw a real spaghetti-bender. I had a double order of everything, and that was only as an appetizer. Jerry still doesn't believe the performance he witnessed that night.

I met these guys quite by accident. I had no idea Bob Keiss or Jerry Coyle even existed, since they did their training on Belle Isle in Detroit at seven o'clock in the morning and I don't even go to Belle Isle at seven o'clock at night. What's a Boston Marathon anyway?

One day I was doing one of those off-the-top-of-your-head columns about things I'd like to do before I died (hit a home run over the left-field wall at Fenway Park, take Natalie Wood to dinner, eat breakfast with Natalie Wood) when a sudden thought popped into my brain: "I'd like to cover the Boston Marathon before I die."

I did this because of something Stan Issacs once told me. Stan is a columnist for *Newsday* on Long Island. He told me I could never consider myself a complete—compleate?—sportswriter until I covered the Boston Marathon.

So I threw out the line, and figured it was a throwaway, when here comes a letter from Dr. Gerald Coyle, D.D.S. It was a nice letter. Very warm. Very sincere. Jerry had noticed my line about the Marathon and so he enclosed a booklet on the race in case I ever got to Boston. He felt this would give me some idea of what it was about.

As it turned out, I was assigned to my first Marathon only a few weeks later (1975) and because I didn't know where to start I hauled out Jerry's book and read it from cover to cover.

I was surprised. It was quite interesting. I didn't know what those guys had to go through to run that crazy distance. I had trouble making it up the stairs; here they were running 26 miles and 385 yards.

But I wanted to "humanize" my stories on the Marathon. So I asked around and found out that there was a guy out at the Detroit Institute of Technology—the athletic director—who ran in the Boston Marathon every year. So I called up Bob Keiss and asked could I come out and talk to him.

Again, I was delightfully surprised. I thought he was going to bore me to tears with endless bleating of the great sacrifices these courageous men had to make to run in this hallowed race.

Naw. Bob told me he took a portable radio along with him to listen to the Red Sox game from Fenway Park, and immediately I knew I would like this man, and maybe even his race. I had no idea Bob and Jerry knew each other—and it wasn't until we were on the plane to Boston, where we were all thrown together— I got the connection. They were great friends and beautiful people and I began learning about the Boston Marathon and all of its majesty.

The press bus never finished. It stalled at the top of the hill coming down to Prudential Center and we got booed by the crowd as we got out and hurried down to the finish line. Here these

47

people had waited for hours to see the finish of the race and now this big bus broke down in front of them and blocked their view. As I recall, it was the only booing I heard all day long, a rare circumstance in the city of Boston.

Anyway, I got hooked that year and hooked good. Everybody was a story. Everybody had something to say. For the first time in my life I had to purposely make myself leave the scene of a sporting event because I was getting too much material. Had I stayed at the finish line another hour, I would have been burdened with so much copy I would have never gotten it all written.

I was not able to make the 1976 running of the Marathon because of a torn tendon in my left leg. In fact, I spent Patriots' Day in St. Joseph's Hospital in Ann Arbor. I knew where my thoughts were—and my sentiments, too.

So, trying to be a good reporter, I did the next best thing. I asked Bob and Jerry if they would take a tape recorder with them and just put down their thoughts. Nothing big. Nothing important. Just what they saw and felt.

"We're not newspapermen," said Jerry.

"I know that. Just talk into the recorder."

Bob Keiss speaking . . .

"April 16, 1976. It's six A.M. and normally I'd be getting out to run by now but I'm getting all my things together and putting them in the suitcase for the trip to Boston.

"Now I'm wondering—should I check my bag or carry it aboard the plane? I've got my running shoes in the bag and that's the one thing I can't do without. I don't need that extra coat, that extra tie or that shirt. But I can't afford to lose my shoes.

"It was awfully crowded in the airport parking lot. We took a bus over to the terminal and the guy is driving like mad. I'm thinking to myself, 'Hey, man, slow down. I don't want to train for eight weeks and then wind up in an accident.'

"Okay, we're checking in. Where'd all these people come from? They're surely not all going to Boston to run in the Marathon.

"Hey, watch it, buddy. Don't push that suitcase up against my Achilles' tendon. I don't need that at all. I've had this fractured arm for three weeks now and that's enough to worry about. I'm glad I brought Mary Ann along. She can carry the heavy suitcases.

"I've just looked at the three-day forecast for Michigan. It says

against my shoes. I've gotten blisters everywhere you can think of on my feet but it's better without the socks.

"My number is 162. Jerry's number is 278—the same as my extension at work. I ought to be able to remember that. We're going down to Jerry's room now for breakfast. I'll turn it over to Jerry, since he's the real talker on this team."

Jerry Coyle speaking . . .

"Bob and I had a date to meet in my room, which we've done for years, since we didn't want to fight the crowds down in the rest of the hotel. We decided to bring our own stuff and it's a very simple matter. We hooked up a small electric coffee pot so we could heat up some water. We went out the day before and bought some instant coffee, some instant oatmeal, a couple of grapefruit, some muffins and jelly and that kind of stuff. He came by at about eight o'clock and we just plugged in everything and started eating— instant coffee, instant oatmeal, muffins, grapefruit, the whole thing, and it was just great. We were loading up on those carbohydrates just as we wanted to. The buses were due to leave at about nine-thirty so we just sat around and gabbed. We had a couple of bran muffins, which stimulates the old lower colon, and so just before we left the room each of us had our monumental bowel movement, which is always a great relief on the morning of the race. It's a lot better than having it in Framington or some place like that, so we took care of that and then went downstairs and got on one of the buses which would take us out to Hopkinton.

"It was a pretty typical ride. One of the things that keeps going through your mind, the Goddamned bus keeps going and going and you can't believe he's going out there only twenty-six miles. It seems like he's going from Boston to Baltimore. I'm sitting next to this guy from Philadelphia, a physician, and this is his first Boston Marathon. He's really getting shook up with the distance we're traveling and I keep assuring him that we're taking the long way around and that we don't have to run as long as this bus was driving. Most of the time we just sat there chewing the fat about our training procedures and that sort of thing. I could see all of his apprehensions and I was trying to soothe him down.

"We finally pulled into Hopkinton and this is where the excitement really starts to set in. You get that little tingle as you step off the bus. The whole town is starting to come alive. This is their big day, the one day of the year when the whole world looks upon Hopkinton, Massachusetts. They don't do another damned thing for three-hundred and sixty-four days but for this one moment, this is their moment just as it is our moment, and Hopkinton is all alive.

"The people are out. The flags are out. Bands are playing. Balloons. Girl Scouts selling cookies. The people. The crowds. The traffic. You feel it all around. We wend our way to the gymnasium and now you realize you are there. A lot of runners are already dressed in their suits, already warming up. It's hard to believe all the people. You see the Japanese for the first time and the Koreans and the South Africans and the Mexicans. White and black, every size and shape and age. Little kids. TV cameras. Writers everywhere, mingling with the runners, getting their quotes. Pictures are being taken. Friends are taking pictures of loved ones. You just feel the vastness of the whole thing. It is all around you.

"Going inside, going into the gym, is a special experience. Guys all over the place. Guys taping feet, taping toes. Band-Aids all over. Putting Vaseline into their shoes, making makeshift headbands, trying to pin numbers on. God, it's small in that place, and the smell. All that liniment. The odor. You'd think a dinosaur was being treated for a pulled hamstring.

"You see faces from other years and some you never saw before. I saw Joe Pardo, a blind runner from Flushing, New York, and, gee, I was delighted to see Joe. Joe is kind of an interesting guy. He's fifty-four now and about four years ago, Bob and I were running and we saw this guy running with a white cane. He had a guy running along with him but the guy was getting pretty tired. As we came up to them, he said, 'You guys gonna finish?' We said, 'Sure, we're going to make it.' He said, 'Would you mind helping my friend?' 'Sure, sure, fine, anything you say.' So Bob got on one side of Joe and I got on the other and we gave him directions. He was glowing—God, the faith in that man. To put himself—his whole safety—in the hands of two total strangers he never met before and probably would never meet again . . . I'll tell you, that was some feeling. Here we are, three men, three runners, thrown together on the back roads of Massachusetts. And so we led the way for him. 'Turn left, Joe . . . turn right now, Joe. Watch it! You're edging over now. Joe—get back! Get back! Watch out for that curb now, Joe. We're crossing railroad tracks now, Joe. Pick up your feet.' We got him water and that sort of thing. We got up and down the hills and went right into Boston with him. It was such a thrill, the three of us crossing the finish line holding hands. You see, there are a lot of things about Joe. He had a son who was killed in Vietnam. Joe was a former Detroiter. Just by coincidence, he spent a couple of years at Catholic Central and so we knew a lot of the same people. Because he had some relatives in Detroit, his boy was buried in Mt. Olivet Cemetery. Joe had never seen the grave. Never *seen* the grave? What am I saying? He had never *been* to the grave, never visited it. So on Good Friday, like the Friday before we went to Boston, I took a ride out to Mt. Olivet Cemetery. I had a camera with me and went to the office and got directions and found Tom Pardo's grave. I bought a small American flag and a bouquet of flowers and placed them on the grave and then I took some pictures from different angles. I took a close-up shot of the headstone and I told Joe about this . . . that I had visited his son's grave and that I'd taken some pictures . . . and he really appreciated that. He said, 'Oh, jeez, great Jerry! I'll really be anxious to see those pictures.' I told him, 'Okay, Joe, I know what you mean.' So I described the grave site to him. I told him what trees were there. Joe went blind at the age of twenty-seven and so he remembered the intersection of Van Dyke and East Six Mile and he remembered Outer Drive and City Airport. As I described the grave, just where it was, he is saying, 'Yeah, yeah, Jerry. I know just where you mean.' I said, 'There are three beautiful Michigan pines there, Joe right near the grave. He is buried on a little knoll and there's a beautiful blossoming tree right there.' I wasn't sure what kind it was but it had red blossoms on it and I said, 'Joe, it's just gorgeous. It's a very beautiful sight.' He kept listening and nodding his head and saying, 'Yeah, Jerry, yeah.'

"That was one guy I ran into. Then there was a one-armed guy that I'd seen in the past. Gus. I don't know his last name. I'd see him only once a year but I'd go up to him and say, 'Hi, Gus.' And he'd smile and say, 'How are you today?' He was a guy of fifty-five or sixty and even though I saw him only this one time, we were pals. And then there'd be old Johnny Kelley. You'd always see him. He'll be roaming around in there, and there are usually a couple of reporters following him. And you'd see all the college kids, all of them getting so excited. Man, they've got more gimmicks than you can think of. They've got tape—I saw one kid who taped every toe individually, then taped his entire foot, then put on his socks and then his shoes. It was the damndest thing I saw in my whole life. Others were Vaselining up—areas of abrasion, where constant rubbing will cause rashes and bleeding. You always Vaseline up the crotch and the nipples because, hey, they can really tear you up. I remember once running in a marathon, I think it was on Belle Isle in Detroit, I had on a white T-shirt and I have pictures of it. I forgot to tape my nipples and it looks like I'm wearing No. 11. The bloodstains, one from each nipple, are dripping down the front of my shirt, two red lines, looking like I'm No. 11. Some people put Vaseline on their eyebrows. When you perspire and the sweat comes running down, the Vaseline sort of makes a little dam. The sweat will kind of trickle off to one side rather than go through the hair and into your eyes. So they've got all these gimmicks and then there's the nervous pee. Jeez, they line up at that john, all the way down the hall, some of the guys doing a dance as they wait their turn. They've probably emptied their bladder half a dozen times already but there's that one last nervous pee that they have to take. I've got a favorite little spot. It's right behind a bush, about halfway between the gymnasium and the starting line. I found this place and I'm not telling too many people about it, so I save mine for there.

"It's stuffy in the gym now, especially this time, and I wanted to get out of there. I got separated from my wife, and the other kids but I've got my son Pat, who's fourteen years old, with me. He's a curious little guy, a good athlete, too. Loves to swim. He was in the gymnasium with me and, boy, his eyes were bugging out like saucers as he looked around at all the excitement in there.

"When we went outside, the first guy I saw was George Sheehan of New Jersey. He's a cardiologist and he was being interviewed by one of the Boston TV stations. George was telling them about the heat and his line was, 'This is a day of survival. That's all we're thinking about. We're not thinking of records, we're not thinking of personal goals. Finishing. That's all that's on our minds today.' I listened for a while because I felt that way, too. We just had to survive. It was one hundred degrees—give or take five degrees—and you could feel the heat baking up from the ground. On a day like this, you should wear something light—something light in weight and light in color. Bob and I had pink caps, which were ideal, because they were light in weight and light in color. The cap also had a peak to shade your eyes from the sun and you could put ice cubes under the cap and they'd be sealed up in there. The water would drip down over your head and keep the blood cool that runs through those cells. You should wear cotton, never nylon. Nylon produces heat. And certainly, nothing like sweat suits or rubberized jackets. Those are really insane.

"We went down past the gas station and were headed for the starting line when we met Larry Power. He's a physician from Ann Arbor and Larry is a good guy. He's got a good sense of humor and so he's playing it pretty cool, even though this is only his second Boston Marathon. He's gagging it up as we walk along and now it's only a half hour before the start of the race and we see this guy and he's gone up to the side of a house and he's got the garden hose on and is letting it pour all over his head. He's taking a cold shower from the hose and I mean he's completely drenched. What good was that going to do him a half hour before the race? But that's what he was doing—that's what people do before the start of this race.

"I found my little bush and slipped in there and I told Pat I was going to have my private pee. When I came out, we ran into Neil O'Connor, another friend from Detroit. Neil is a nervous kind of guy. He was worried. He was saying, 'Let's see . . . let's see if I've got everything. Vaseline? Yeah. Head covering? Yeah. Gatorade? Yeah.' He goes on and on like this and Larry Power looks at him and says, 'Neil, did you remember to turn off the stove?'

"We walk along a little more and there's Bob sitting on the curb with some of the other runners from Detroit, Jeanne and Jerry Bocci and Alexa and Martin Kraft, two husband-and-wife teams that were running. So I stopped for a moment and there's all this goddamned goofy chatter going on. All this nervous bullshit. This is the last thing I need fifteen minutes before the Boston Marathon. I say to myself, 'Man, I got to get out of here,' so I walk away with Pat and look for a quiet place for myself. I guess everybody does it a little differently. I want a little time by myself. I can feel the adrenalin starting to run and I don't need all that nervous chatter. Maybe some people respond by being glib. Or maybe they're giving out with caustic comments. Or they're trying to slough it off with their quasi-humor. Maybe some of them make light of the whole thing and that's the way they hide their feelings. I've seen guys get so excited they literally wet their pants. Other guys' teeth will start chattering. Some of them will get goose bumps. I like to be quiet. It's okay if I'm talking on a one-to-one basis, but I find myself getting a little philosophical and I like to be by myself. It was this way when I was playing football at the University of Detroit. I would be fine getting dressed . . . I could talk with our coach, but once we got out on the field, once we were ready to play, I'd kind of sit on the bench by myself and get ready. It was almost like something was festering in me. This is just my way and I suppose I'll never change.

"I've still got Pat with me and we go between two houses to get into the shade. We're standing there—and Pat's a pretty perceptive kid. He said to me, 'You did'nt like all that talk over there, did you?' I said, 'No Pat, not really. I'd rather be over here with you—just the two of us. You know Pat, I'm a pretty lucky guy to have a son who will stand here with me as I'm getting ready to run in the Boston Marathon . . . somebody I can really share my thoughts with. You kind of give me strength. If I don't want to talk, you understand. That's because we know each other so well.'

"The kid looks up at me and says, 'Dad, is this like getting butterflies?'

" 'Exactly,' I tell him. 'You're a pretty smart feller for a fourteen-year-old.'

"He said, 'Do you get 'em in the stomach?'

"Yeah, I get 'em in the stomach. It's just like when you're up on the starting block before the start of a hundred-meter freestyle.'

"Pat looks up at me and says, 'Yeah, I know just what you mean.'

"We're standing there when this big Japanese delegation comes over to get into the shade too. I don't speak any Japanese but I learned one word that's kind of universal in Japan. It's 'O-HI-O' just like in Columbus, Ohio, which means 'good morning' or 'good day.' So when this Japanese guy comes over, I smile at him and he gives me a big toothy grin and kind of a half bow. I say, 'O-HI-O' and he lights up so that you can't believe it. He starts jabbering away in Japanese and I tell him, 'No, no, no, no.' He stopped and kind of laughed. He realized that was all I knew. I said to him, 'Tokyo? . . . Yokohama? . . .' and now he says, 'No, no, no, no. Osaka' I try to tell him 's-h-i-p, I sail a big ship to Japan' and he says, 'Ahhhhhh, ship.' I tell him, 'hot.' I brush off the sweat from my brow. He steps back into the sun and says, 'Hot.' Now he steps back into the shade and smiles. It's just amazing—here we are, a couple of guys, just standing there trading a few words and a lot of sign language, but we knew exactly what each other meant. You get that gut feeling. You get that feeling of, 'Man, I understand. I understand.' We're both going to try to do this damned thing and we both knew we were going to bust our butts out there. You've been through it before, I've been through it before, so we understand. We have a common bond. We know about the challenges, the threats, the hidden dangers, all the tests along the way. And we know about the exhilaration, too, of finishing the race. Just two guys who may never meet again, from opposite sides of the world —only for a few minutes, just sharing our feelings. I guess maybe that's what it's all about.

"Pat is watching this whole scene and I can see the excitement in his face. 'Boy, dad,' he says, 'do you think someday I could run in the Boston Marathon?'

"I said, 'Sure. You're as good an athlete as I know. You're just the kind of guy who can do it. You're a tough little snot. And you'll train. You set your mind to this thing—you bet your life you can run it. It'll be the greatest thing in the world to run with you.'

"He said, 'Boy, Dad, that would be great. When can we do it?'

" 'Well,' I told him, 'you've got to be eighteen. That's only four years from now. We'll do it, just the two of us.'

"This was just the kind of atmosphere I needed. It's now about five minutes before the start, so we head out into the street. I give Pat my pack and he's kind of a sentimental little kid. He's like so many of us crazy Irish. Sentimental. Sensitive. Emotional. The big thing about us Irish is that our kidneys are built too close to our eyes. So as I was standing there, I happened to look over at Pat just as the gun went off. The little guy made a fist and said, 'Good luck, Dad.' I said, 'Aw, thanks, Pat. I really needed that.' I could see a little tear in his eye and I'll tell you I had to swallow a few times myself.

"So now we're ready to move. It's here and you know that all the problems are real, the heat, the challenge of twenty-six, never really knowing if you've done enough training . . . or even if you have, you never know what can go wrong out there. You can't go into this race cocky. You might be able to run the Boston Marathon but you never really beat the course. It's like, I suppose, a father. He allows you certain latitudes. But don't try to embarrass him. Don't take away his authority. The Boston Marathon has a personality of its own. It's there and it's real, and you can see it and you can feel it. It's big. It's prestigious. It's sensitive. It's kind of loving. And it's welcoming. He allows you in on this special day. He greets you with a smile. But don't ever insult him. Don't ever get cocky. He'll just stand up and slap you across the face. It's kind of like God, I guess. Just don't screw around too much or He's going to knock you right on your ass. Don't ever think you can get away with too much. Don't ever think you've conquered this course. It'll slap you down so fast it'll make your head spin.

"The field is starting to surge forward and now I'm looking for Bob. He's about six yards ahead of me, but I can't get up to him. There is a mob of people between us. So he sort of hangs back and waits for me. You really don't run in the first fifty yards. You sort of shuffle, or walk, or even come to a stop. For the first few miles, it's kind of an intense race. You're dodging people all along the way. Some are passing you, and you're passing a few. You're more concerned with the traffic than anything else. You can't get into any rhythm for the first four or five miles. The course is rolling up and down and it's twisting from side to side but this doesn't bother you very much. It's staying out of the way of the other runners—that's the problem.

"One of the first things we look for—about three or four miles out—is this farm on the right-hand side of the road. It's set up on some rolling terrain, a beautiful old place and it has a stone fence in front of it. It's like a cobblestone fence that seems to go on endlessly. It weaves in and out like the waves of the ocean and they've got this big field up there, this meadow, and there are some horses up there. They are the most beautiful horses you have ever seen in your life. They look like Thoroughbreds. They're frisky and they're prancing about, as if they know just how good they look. They're young and they're vivacious and they're just having one helluva good time. We always look for these horses and so it was a disappointment this time when we didn't see them. I felt a little let down. But then I thought to myself, 'Hey, maybe they were feeling the heat, too. Maybe they were using a little of their horse sense and staying put in that barn instead of coming out in all that sun. So we missed the horses this time and then, a little later, I noticed Frank Stranahan going right by us.

"Now, you can always pick out Frank. He runs in the most beautifully tailored suit that was ever made. A custom-made T-shirt with a neat collar that fits him just perfectly. Frank's the former golfer. He used to play as an amateur on the circuit. He comes out of that Toledo, Ohio, fortune and he gave up golf and took up running. He's down to about one hundred fifty-five pounds now. He's a vegetarian and he's on a health kick. I've run with Frank in the past and he's a nice guy. He doesn't miss golf one bit. He can't stand the game. Here's a guy whose total life was a commitment to golf. He played it as a kid and played it well. Nobody could hit the ball farther off the tee than Frank Stranahan. I think he won the L.A. open as an amateur, but now the game means nothing to him. He comes right by and you can't miss him in the peaked cap and that million-dollar outfit. He's wearing black leotards, of all things—black leotards! Whenever I see him in those damned things . . . well, Bob and I will run up behind him and I'll say, 'You know, Coach, I wonder if Frank Stranahan is going to run this year?' Bob will say, 'Yeah, we'll probably see him somewhere along the way.' I'll say, 'I wonder if he's done anything about the poor circulation in his legs?' Bob will say, 'Yeah, the last time we saw him his legs were all black.' 'Yeah,' I'll say, 'he's got bad blood, man. He's just got bad wheels. All black. He looks just terrible.' Of course this always gets a little rise out of Frank, but, you understand, we can do these things because it's still early in the race.

"As I say, we're at about the four- or five-mile mark and we're not in automatic yet. But here comes Stranahan running right by us and I look at Bob and say, 'He's going too fast, Coach. Much too fast.' I mean, it's hot out here and it's going to be a real survival test. Forget 3:15. Forget 3:20. Forget 3:30. We're out here to finish and nothing more. When we reach the twelve- or thirteen-mile mark, we see a pickup truck and they've got about thirty runners on the back—guys who had thrown in the towel—and sitting on the side of the truck was Frank Stranahan. That proved our point and made us realize that we'd better stick with our original philosophy.

"Another thing had happened that made us think. It was around the five-mile mark when we saw this young kid—he looked like a college student—and he was out cold on the side of the road. He was laying there on his back. I didn't get a good look at him so I couldn't tell exactly what kind of trouble he was in. But the thought went through my mind about a story I read about a runner running in, oh, a ten- or twelve-mile race, and he dropped to the ground unconscious after only five miles. His coach immediately began attending to him. The runner had wet and clammy skin, which was a symptom of heat exhaustion. Heat exhaustion, not heatstroke. They are two entirely different matters. You can treat heat exhaustion but you can die of heatstroke. So this kid has the symptoms of heat exhaustion but you can go from one to the other, from heat exhaustion into heatstroke. The kid's skin then got very hot and very red. He began running a high temperature and this is exactly what was happening to him. He went from heat exhaustion to heatstroke and he died. So I'm thinking of this kid lying on the side of the road and I'm saying, 'hey, we're only five miles out and they're dropping already.' In fact, as I found out later, the first one to go down was a runner from West Germany. He fell after only two miles. Two miles! They rushed him to the hospital—God, you could hear those sirens all day long—and they had to put him into an intensive care unit. He almost died, too, but they brought him out of it. So I knew this was going to be a very serious day, so let's pay attention to what we're doing.

"This was the first startling thought I had. We still hadn't gotten into our so-called pace but we ran on through Ashland and came to Framingham. It's always kind of stimulating to get to Framingham. We're running alongside the railroad tracks and there's a couple of bars there and the guys always come out and give you a big hoopla as you go by. This time I noticed something. They were standing in the shade. They had their beers with them, but they were standing in the shade and they were kind of quiet. We were getting constant reminders like this and, boy, we were starting to feel it already. Normally we don't start taking in fluids until the six- or seven-mile mark but this time were taking them two or three miles out. As you know, Bob carries that radio with him and we each had a bottle of ERG—electrolyte replacement glucose. It's something like Gatorade—it replaces the electrolytes you lose through perspiration.

"I noticed something else. A lot of people were offering water and orange slices sooner in the race. You'd usually get these a few miles down the road but they were there almost from the start. I was taking the water but not the orange slices. Even though there was glucose there, there was a certain amount of acid in the oranges and I thought that might create a problem, so I left them alone. I kept putting ice cubes under my hat.

"The people were out with their hoses and it got to be an incredible scene. It was almost like a war effort. You'd see whole teams—whole families—working to help the runners. The father would be directing these teams. 'Get that next bucket out here! More ice cubes, more ice cubes!' The wife would have half a dozen sponges. She'd throw them to the runners. You'd take one and squeeze the cold water over your head, then drop it to the ground. The wife would send a kid out to pick up the sponge and she'd put it back into the bucket of ice water. These people were *involved!* It was almost like a mission. This was a complete commitment. This was Patriots' Day and this is what you did on Patriots' Day. No questions asked. These runners needed help and you just did it.

"At first, I didn't want to get that wet. I wasn't as concerned about the upper part of my body as I was of getting the water down into my socks, then into my shoes. That could create a real problem. I wanted to keep my shoes as dry as possible. Heat plus water creates friction—and then you've got blisters. I didn't want that at all.

"As we came to a hose, I'd point to the top of my body. 'Here. Up here.' They'd squirt it over my head and shoulders. I noticed the kids with their cups of water. They knew something was up, too. As you came by, they wouldn't hand you the cups as they usually did. They'd throw the water on you, figuring that's what you really needed. God love the people of Boston.

"It's kind of interesting . . . up until Wellesley, which is the thirteen-mile mark, or even Newton, at fifteen miles . . . when they squirted you with the water, you could feel it. Not only the pressure of the water but the coldness. It created a definite sensation and it made you feel good. You felt exhilarated when that cold water hit you. It made you tingle and woke you up for a moment.

"But then, around Wellesley and Newton, I just couldn't feel that coldness any more. You knew they were squirting you. You could feel the force of the water as it ran down your body, but it wasn't that exhilarating any more. I started to wonder about this. Hey, why don't I feel that cold any more? Am I losing sensitivity here? Am I losing neurological response? I remember taking those ice cubes in the early part of the race and putting them under my hat, dripping down and cooling off my face. I'd take one and put it behind my neck and hold it there. I could feel the cold and it felt good. Now I was doing the same thing, putting the ice cubes on

61

the back of my neck but I might as well have been holding a rock back there. I could't feel anything. It was very strange.

"Running along—maybe at sixteen or seventeen miles—I remember where I got kind of dizzy. I had some blurred vision and this can be a very serious thing. I felt a little nauseous, like I wanted to throw up. These are some of the symptoms you get when you get heatstroke. Dizziness. High temperature. Rapid pulse. Delirium. I began slowing the pace and Bob, without realizing it, started pulling ahead of me. We have kind of a pact to stick together, as long as it's a comfortable run. But hey, if one guy falls back— then it's every man for himself. Run your own race. You have to do what you have to do. You do your best. So I said, 'Hey, Coach, I'm not feeling so good. I'm really hurting. You better go on ahead.' Bob Keiss never said bullshit in his life but that's what he was thinking: 'Hey, no way. What do I have to prove? Let's just slow 'er down a bit.' He told me to walk a few steps. I did. I stopped running and started walking. Wow, I was really kind of flaky. I walked maybe ten or fifteen yards and I thought, jeez, if I keep doing this, I'm only going to get sicker.' And the last thing I wanted to do was sit down. You know how it is when you feel sick, like maybe you're going to throw up. You think if you keep moving around, keep swallowing, that it'll go away. I guess maybe I knew too much. I mean about heat exhaustion and heatstroke. I thought maybe this isn't my day. Maybe you're not going to make it. Maybe this is the day you throw it in and get on that losers' truck. This is a blow to your pride but at this point I was feeling panicky. Like pride didn't mean too much any more. I thought, am I really going to hurt myself? What do I need this for? Am I going to kill myself? I thought about all of these things and—don't ask me why—but I started running again. I figured that, if nothing else, it would make me forget about my nausea.

"What I didn't know—what I didn't realize until later—is how much we were laboring. We decided to lay back. Lay off the pace. If it took us four-and-a-half hours to finish, fine. But survive. That's what we were attempting to do. Survive.

"The run into Wellesley is always stimulating, with the gals out there giving us the big hoopla. This time I noticed there wasn't quite the enthusiasm on the part of the runners—it wasn't quite the same as in other years. We'd always chitchat with the gals. We'd talk to them and they'd holler back: 'Come on Detroit!' 'Come on Motown.' 'Go get 'em, Doctor!' This year . . . we just weren't too talkative. I'm really starting to feel it at Wellesey and Bob recognized this. So he became determined that there was no way he was going to run away from me. He was going to keep us BOTH going! This is a real super star, this Keiss. He's a true friend, let me tell you. He could see me getting down, so he started talking to all the people, carrying on a running conversation all along the way: 'God bless you, Boston!' 'Hooray for you, Boston!' 'Thanks for the water!' 'Hey there, Charlie—how're you doing!' Of course it was all for my benefit. But that's the kind of guy Bob is.

"I remember one time, about three or four years ago, when I was having a real bad day in Boston, he literally dragged me in. I don't know when I ever hurt so much in my life. When we finished, he got me into a cab and we went across town to the Parker House Hotel where we were staying. I never had such intense pain in my body before. I was almost crying I was in such agony. Bob got me out of the cab and up to the room. He filled the tub with warm water and lifted me—literally lifted me—into the tub. I couldn't move. He would submerge one leg in the warm water and then lift it out and wrap it in cold towels that he got from the sink. Then he'd submerge the other leg, then lift it out and wrap it in cold towels. Then the first leg went back into warm water and so on and on. He did this for a full half hour, maybe forty-five minutes— lifting one leg, lowering the other, going from hot to cold to hot to cold. He sent our wives downstairs for some honey and tea and some potato chips to replace the salt in my body. That big ape took care of me when I couldn't take care of myself. When he finally got me on my feet so I could walk around the room, he started to take care of himself. Later that evening, his wife, Mary Ann, said to him: 'Bob, that was a great thing you did today but how could you do something like that after running twenty-six miles yourself?' And then Bob gave her what I've always called a classic line. He said: 'Mary Ann, only one of us can hurt at a time.' In other words, he couldn't hurt until he made sure I was okay.

"So again he had to drag me through this race. As I think back on it, the whole thing was a little frightening. I know that course like I know the back of my hand, but I just don't remember running parts of it. That's real scary. I've tried to remember running past this landmark or that landmark, but it's a complete blank to me.

"Heartbreak Hill. I'd like to say it was murderous but I don't remember too much about it. I guess it's because we were going so slow it didn't matter if we were going up the hills or down the hills. I do remember one thing—that cop standing on the top of the hill with his bullhorn: 'Congratulations! You have just conquered Heartbreak Hill! Good luck! It's less than five miles to go and it's all downhill.' That was a bunch of crap—all downhill—but I do remember that. When we go to the top of the hill, there were two Jesuits standing there watching us. As I ran by, I said, 'Hey, man, don't just stand there smoking that pipe. Get in there and say a few Aves.'

"Bob was still at it! 'Thanks Boston! Thanks for waiting for us!' 'You saved the day, Boston.' 'You're great, Boston! You're great!' J saw one old guy—he must have been in his seventies—and he was holding a small American flag, the kind you buy on a stick. He was giving us a small ovation—clapping softly, like . . . clap . . . clap clap. He said: 'Keep going, young man. You're doing just fine.' I looked at him and thought to myself: 'Thanks, pops. I really needed that.'

"I guess I can be a sentimental slob at times. At times like these I can get to be a little melancholy, a little philosophical. I never run in Boston but that I don't think of my dad. My father was a dentist, an old farm boy from up in Canada. He left the farm to come down to Assumption College in Windsor, just across the river from Detroit. He and I practiced together the last ten years of his life. He died when he was almost eighty-one years old. He was the greatest man I've ever known. He was just a marvelous individual. He was kind, he had wit, he was a historian, he had gab, he was sensitive, tough, hardworking, cultured and honest. He was also a fine dentist and a great storyteller. Being Canadian he used to tell us stories about one of his favorite people—the Indian Tom Longboat: 'Ohhhhh, Tom Longboat. He would run without shoes. You kids don't know how lucky you are. Poor Tom. He was an Indian boy. He had no shoes. He lived on a reservation. He had no shoes. He would have to hitch rides to run in his races. But he would run and he would win.' Actually, Tom Longboat did win the Boston Marathon in 1907. But my dad—who always had a little of the Irish blarney in him—he'd always call him 'The great Tom Longboat.' So I always had this mystique about running in the Boston Marathon. When I first started thinking about running in Boston

64

about eight or nine years ago, I thought what a thrill it would be if I could take my father—Mom and Pop—to Boston to see this race. Unfortunately the poor guy died in December 1967 and I ran my first Marathon in April 1968. I always think of him during the race and I try to make him a part of it, if I can. So, as I was laboring along, I thought about my dad . . . and it kind of helped me to keep going.

"You see, there is also a great enjoyment about this race—a great feeling of satisfaction. That's when you get down to that last mile. That's when you know you've made it. That's when you know you've paid the price. The last mile is fun. You kind of relax and enjoy it. Your pace picks up a little. You get a skip to your stride. Your head comes up. You start to smile a little and start kibitzing with the people. This is when all the happiness starts to set in. You think of all the training, the rain, the snow, the sleet, the heat, up and down hills. You think of all the places you ran. Belle Isle, Derby Hill, the neighborhood, the Y.M.C.A. track. It all leads up to this day, this race . . . this final mile.

"And it all passes so quickly.

"I suppose it's like a wedding day. You plan for it, wait for it and you want to remember every little detail about it. And then it's over so quickly. Sometimes I wish that last mile would last forever, but you know it's going to be over in another seven or eight minutes, maybe nine. So you try to savor it, remember every bit of it.

"I really don't know how those people can still be out there when we come to the finish line. They've been there for four whole hours! How can they still have that enthusiasm, that feeling for you? I just don't know. They stand there and they applaud, and my God, their hands must be raw by now. But they keep saying: 'Come on . . . come on. You can make it. You're almost there. Come on.'

"It's strange . . . you don't have to talk to them but they know how you feel. I remember one guy. He was big—I mean big. Big and burly, like the roughest, toughest teamster or longshoreman you'd ever want to meet. He was standing there holding a can of beer. He didn't say anything and I didn't say anything but our eyes met for an instant. Just an instant. But in that moment I knew exactly what was on his mind. He was saying: 'Hey, I understand. I appreciate what you are doing. I think you've got balls. Some guys may think you're kooky, but I think you're okay. I understand.'

"So what is the Boston Marathon? I don't know. We run in other places in other races but nothing is like Boston. There is just something special about Boston.

"It's the people. It's the history. It's the tradition. It's the mystique.

"It's the people."

8
"Mr. DeMarathon"

CLARENCE H. DEMAR won the Boston Marathon more times than any man in history—1911, 1922, 1923, 1924, 1927, 1928, 1930. Seven times in all. In his own way he was every bit as much a giant as Ruth, Grange, Tilden, Sande or any of the other legendary figures of The Roaring Twenties. And yet, he was largely unknown—for the Boston Marathon had not caught on in America as yet. People spent more time watching marathon dancing than marathon running. DeMar was a sober man, very serious, very stern—very strict. It is strange that he was portrayed in so light a manner by Dave Egan, the celebrated "Colonel" of Boston sports writing, in this gay era of the 1920s:

By David Egan
Boston Globe Sports Writer

Clarence H. DeMar broke more hearts in 2h 34m 48s than Peggy Hopkins Joyce in her whole life.

*　　*　　*

His legs may not be as shapely as Claudette Colbert's, but they are equally famous.

*　　*　　*

67

"Thank you," said Clarence to the B.A.A. officials when the race was over, "for giving me a chance to get some exercise." Ho-hum!

*   *   *

As soon as this DeMar boy gets a little experience, he's going to be a fair sort of runner.

*   *   *

Where are all these young pups who usually pop up "bearing the torch of flaming youth"? DeMar must have snuffed out their candles.

*   *   *

Many of the prize pecans started with a lemon in one hand, but I imagine even a lemon would get heavy if you had to carry it 26 miles 385 yards.

*   *   *

Instead of calling it the B.A.A. Marathon, it should simply be called DeMarathon.

*   *   *

DeMar planned to run the distance in 2 hours and 32 minutes and was three minutes behind schedule. Just young and irresponsible, I suppose.

*   *   *

Somebody suggested that it was a great day for the Irish when Kyronen and Koski kame klattering klubwards. DeMar destroyed dem.

*   *   *

They say water and gasoline won't mix, but DeMar drank water and inhaled gasoline fumes all along the route.

*   *   *

It was rumored that if DeMar wishes to compete in any B.A.A. Marathon, he will have to run with an old-fashioned safe on his back.

This is about as funny as life ever got for Clarence H. DeMar. He was a humorless man, bitter at times and—according to one account—"almost venomous in his old days."

Yet the hold that DeMar had on the Boston Marathon, and indeed all of Boston, was so powerful that a Dave Egan could present him in a light manner and get away with it. DeMar was a hero in his way and nobody likes to see heroes exposed for what they truly are. No mud-slinging, not even if your name is Dave Egan.

DeMar was a tremendous athlete, an incomparable long-distance runner. Nobody has ever come close to matching his feats in the Boston Marathon. You can only speculate on how many more races he might have won if a doctor had not warned him of a murmur in his heart. DeMar stayed out nine years—nine peak years—and it is anybody's guess how many titles he would have won from 1912 through 1921 when he merely watched from the sidelines. As it was, when he decided to run again he compiled a string of victories that will probably stand forever. It is difficult enough for anyone to win one Marathon these days. That's because there are so many fine runners. Two in a row is almost unheard of any more. To win seven—forget it. DeMar's record of seven B.A.A. championships— like Cy Young's 511 victories or Lou Gehrig's 2,130 consecutive games—will probably live forever.

In winning his first Marathon in 1911, DeMar ran in spite of his physician's warning that there was something wrong with his heart. The doctor was wrong in his diagnosis and, as late as 1953, at the age of sixty-five, DeMar submitted to a series of exhaustive tests and the examining physicians found not only a perfect heart but one that was so powerful it boggled their minds.

Yet, young Clarence H. DeMar watched for nine years while others ran. He told Jerry Nason later, "I think the doc must have been listening to his own heart."

Finally, he could take no more of the inactivity. He decided if he was to die, he would die doing the thing he loved most in life— running.

Thus began the most stunning string of successes marathon running has ever known. He ran fast, he ran hard; he ran aggressively; he ran with discipline. The truth is, Clarence H. DeMar devoted his entire life to running and the saddest part of his story is that the thing that made him happiest also was the cause of his greatest grief. For he hated the hoopla about the sport—the inevitable glad-handers who were there to greet him at the ending; those who, unable to withstand the rigors of running, would move in and attempt to become a vicarious part of Clarence H. DeMar's life and share in his many triumphs. He was heard to say, in later years, that it was better to finish second or third—up the track somewhere—than to have to go through all that frivolity at the finish line—the picture-taking, the autographs, the back-slapping. Clarence H. DeMar was a very private person and one surmised that his idea of the perfect Boston Marathon would be one without any spectators along the route—none of those silly people throwing water on the runners or giving them orange slices or, worst of all, touching them, slapping them, grabbing them as they came by. Clarence H. DeMar slugged more than one spectator on his way to victory in Boston.

Most of all, he hated those who would tell him how to run—the coaches or trainers who would work with the runners. He was almost paranoid in his dislike for them. He felt they were nothing more than headline-grabbers who thought no more of the runners than they would of dogs eating out of garbage cans in some forsaken alley. Clarence H. DeMar despised them so much that it was the one subject he would discuss for hours. He competed in three Olympics and failed to bring home a medal—even a bronze. He blamed the self-centered coaches, or trainers, for much of his troubles. They just didn't understand running. They sure didn't understand Clarence H. DeMar.

To understand the personality of this man, it is necessary to understand his background. He did not grow up in the most ideal of conditions.

He was born in Madeira, Ohio, one of six children. His father died when young Clarence was eight. With an uncommon determination for one so young, he helped support his mother by peddling small articles in neighboring towns for a handsome profit of fifty cents a day.

At the age of ten, the family moved to Warwick, Massachusetts and shortly afterward young Clarence was placed in the Farm and Trade School on Thompson's Island. His mother no longer could afford him. Clarence was dismayed at being separated from his family, but with his now-familiar determination, he set out to make the most of the situation and wound up graduating as the class valedictorian in 1903.

DeMar was a curious man. While he kept his social contacts— and his words—to a bare minimum, he became a prolific writer. He wrote many articles on marathon running, which he submitted to various magazines. Some were accepted, some were not. He even wrote a book of his life, published in 1936. While he was naturally reticent around others, he was a compulsive writer—drawn to the ink as a moth is to the flame. He ultimately became a printer, a fine one, and earned his living working on the Boston newspapers. He'd often run the Marathon in the afternoon and then report to work that night—literally setting the type of his own victory.

It was in one of his many theses that DeMar himself explained how he became involved in running:

70

It was back in 1901, at the age of 21, when I first became interested in distance running. While attending a smoker at the University of Vermont to pep up enthusiasm for a football game, one of the speakers —a Professor Stetson of the German Department—urged all men to try different sports until they found one they could be a champion at.

He had a theory that every man could be a champion at some sport if he only found the right one. At once I wondered what I could be tops at.

I had led a hard and somewhat squelched life since entering the Farm School at Thompson's Island. While I was there I used to wonder why the black and blue marks inflicted by "trainers of underprivileged youth" made me feel unworthy, while similar bruises received on the football field made me proud.

I had the frequent unanswered question to haunt me, "You're good at books, but why can't you do sports or anything else?"

I felt unworthy to associate with people, except at work, and so I had grown to feel myself as socially inferior. So more than most young men in life, I felt I would have to do something in athletics to really make myself somebody.

So Professor Stetson's challenge stimulated my daydreams that I could become something in life. By a process of elimination, I went out for cross-country. But back in those puritanical days when I was practicing, I felt so ashamed to be seen with so few clothes on that I scuttled out of sight as quickly as possible if I saw anyone out on the road.

DeMar, then, was not driven by any great dream of becoming a champion for the sake of being a champion; he simply wanted to be "accepted" in life. Perhaps this explains his compelling desire to succeed at running and why he could not tolerate less than complete dedication (as with the coaches and trainers) of those who touched his life. How many of them, in the dead of the winter, would run from his home to the railroad depot and then from the depot to work—and do the same coming home? It is possible that every time Clarence H. DeMar ran, he ran with an absolute mission; he had to prove himself worthy in his own eyes before he could gain the acceptance of others. No wonder he was so restive. No wonder he ran so damned fast—and so damned long.

In truth, he never stopped running. He competed until the age of sixty-nine when he ran in a fifteen-kilometer marathon in Bath, Maine. Altogether he ran for forty-nine years. On fifteen occasions he finished in the top ten in the Boston Marathon. He ran his last race in Boston in 1954 at the age of sixty-six. He finished 78th in a field of 113. But he did finish. In all, DeMar participated in more than one thousand marathon runs, including one hundred of twenty-five miles or more.

Right from the beginning he was a self-reliant man. He disliked authoritarianism in any form. He didn't even like the bicyclists riding alongside him in those early races, as was the custom in marathoning.

"That Arthur Palmer," DeMar once said of one of his aides, "I had quite a time of it persuading him to keep quiet as I concentrated on the race. I was engaged in trying to read the degree of my fatigue with the distance yet to be covered and Arthur was very set in his opinion that his conversation would make me forget the fatigue. He felt I would run better if we made a social engagement of it."

Little did poor Arthur Palmer know of Clarence H. DeMar.

Running was not a trifling matter; you trained, you ate the right foods, you got the proper amount of rest—and you shut up all along the way.

Some of DeMar's confrontations with the crowds became almost classic. To his credit, he spoke about them willingly—probably because he thought he was right. He probably was, but how do you tell these spectators of the Boston Marathon not to become part of this great event. They *are* part of the montage that makes this race what it is.

"Once, at Auburndale," DeMar recalled, "I was confronted by a youth with a pencil and book looking for my autograph. Spontaneously, I poked him in the face and ran better for it. Running against time and signing autographs are two feats that cannot be done at the same time."

The cyclists almost drove him insane.

"I always told them," said Clarence, " 'The farther away you get, the better I'll like you.' When one failed to take the hint, I used some forceful language on him and threatened to notify the police, who, by the way, were doing an excellent job of patrolling."

DeMar wanted to run his own race, his own way; anyone who interfered with his set schedule was met with great disdain—like if somebody tried to help out by dousing him with water.

"Knowing their irresponsible enthusiasm, I would shout at them and beg them, 'Please don't throw that water!' At least six times in

one race I wasted my wind. One oldster, who looked like a professional trainer, disregarded my entreaties and deliberately doused
my calves with a dipper of cold water. I wonder how many marathons I must win to make the people respect me enough to recognize that, when I run, I am in supreme command of my destiny."

They just wouldn't listen to Clarence's pleadings—"and I'll tell
you, I landed a good strong one on one bozo's nose and he knows
why."

Later, DeMar told Jerry Nason that he was sorry for punching
out the spectator. "I wish I could find the man and apologize,"
DeMar said. "He meant well but the cold water would have stiffened
my legs like clothespins."

It was the ultimate irony that DeMar would run to gain the acceptance of people—and it was people he had to push away to gain
this acceptance.

So that the record is straight, it should be remembered that
DeMar was a runner and a runner without parallel in the Boston
Marathon. In fairness, this is how he should be judged—on per-
formance, not personality. Not everyone was that ga-ga about Ty
Cobb, either—and he might have been the greatest hitter of all
time. Even Teddy Ballgame had his flaws.

But the record is there, and it is clear, and there has never been
anyone like "Mr. DeMarathon." DeMar died on July 10, 1958, four
days after his seventieth birthday. His body gave way, not his heart.

9
"Everybody Here's Seen Kelley!"

WHEN YOU RUN in the Boston Marathon, you try to do two things:

You try to finish.

You try to finish ahead of old Johnny Kelley.

Old John is sixty-nine now and he is easily the most popular of all runners. He's the one they all wait for. He's the one you'd better beat to the finish line. Once he passes by, the crowds disperse. Once he hits the finish line, most of the spectators go home. He is that much of a hero to the people of Boston.

He is their saint in shining armor. He may have skinny legs and knobby knees, but to those along the route from Hopkinton to the Pru, he is a gallant knight on a giant charger. Johnny Kelley is living proof that nothing really changes in life: We are all eternal. God bless you, Johnny Kelley. We love you, Johnny Kelley.

Johnny Kelley loves it all.

Every inch of this 26-mile 385-yard stage.

"I love running . . . I love the crowds," he says with his green eyes gleaming like emeralds. "It's free expression. I reaffirm myself. If I don't run for two or three days I feel as if something's been stolen from me."

The Boston Marathon was first run in 1897, when William

74

McKinley was President. Kelley has been at it since 1928. He has run in more Boston Marathons than any man in history—forty-five. And he has no intention of stopping. He won in 1935 and again in 1945. He has known the pangs of frustration by finishing second no less than seven times. He has been in the top ten finishers a total of nineteen times, an incredible record. Clarence H. DeMar ran in thirty-three Boston Marathons and was in the top ten fifteen times.

Johnny Kelley is but a bird of a man. He is as sparse as a sparrow. It is a true "happening" every time he runs in this race. People cheer. They shout and throw him kisses. Some of them cry. Johnny Kelley represents many things to many people. Mostly, he represents raw determination—the refusal to quit, and they all admire him for it, for they would like to be as determined as old Johnny.

He is a proud man.

When he was representing the United States in the 1936 Olympics, the German soldiers taunted him. How could this frail man be an athlete? They removed his straw hat and replaced it with a helmet. When the helmet slid down over his eyes, the soldiers laughed hysterically.

"Are you on the United States checker team?" one of them asked.

"I'm a runner," said Kelley defiantly. "I'm a marathoner."

The soldier took a step back.

"They were a lot more polite after that," said Kelley.

Kelley is truly a man of the ages. He does indeed seem eternal. At a banquet in 1969, Ted Williams—jowl-faced and paunchy—leaned over to Kelley and said: "I'd give anything to be in your shape."

But would he? Old John is out there every morning, right after breakfast, running his five miles, his ten miles, sometimes twelve miles. He loves it and never misses a morning on the road.

Johnny Kelley lives in East Dennis, on the unspoiled North Shore of the Cape, about eighty miles from downtown Boston. "No honky-tonk around here," he said. "We got it quiet here, the way we like it. The south shore, that's where they've ruined it with their hot dog stands and pizza parlors. It's Coney Island down there."

Johnny Kelley was not a powerful runner in his day. Nimble was more like it. He lacked the endurance to withstand the rigors of twenty-six miles. How many times he led them into the hills. Or coming out of them. Only to falter in the final miles. "If he had any stamina at all, there is no telling how many Marathons he would have won," said Jerry Nason. "There's no question in my mind but that he would have won seven of them, the same as DeMar—and maybe even nine. But Johnny just didn't have enough stamina."

Actually, Johnny Kelley can sit back and enjoy the fruits of his labor. His record is a majestic one. The affection is deserved.

We spent a splendid afternoon at his home on the Cape—even to driving out among the sand dunes. He showed me his many trophies and his many paintings. I even bought a painting for fifty dollars and it will hang in my home forever.

Old Johnny Kelley talked for five straight hours. Next to running, he likes to do that best . . .

"I don't know if I'm the oldest man ever to run in the Marathon, but I'm close to it. There's Peter Foley of Winchester. He was somewhere in his eighties, just toddling along, when his family made him stop. And there's Marty Cavanaugh in Waltham—he's seventy-seven and he finished a couple of years ago, at the age of seventy-four. But he's dropped out now that he's got to qualify.

"I saw my first Marathon when I was twelve years old. My father took me over to Commonwealth Avenue and here came Frank Zuna —he's just flying down the street. I got all excited and I guess that's when I first got interested in it. I was the oldest of ten kids, so I had to go to work to help. My father was a mailman and he didn't make enough for all us kids, so I used to work in a gas station across the street from my school, pumping gas, greasing, oiling—gas was fifteen cents a gallon then—and I'd just change my clothes on my dinner hour and go over to the field and run. I'd work six to nine at night and I'd do my homework on the desk in the gas station and one of my sisters would bring my dinner down to me on a plate.

"I probably should have done a lot more things in those days. We all make mistakes in life and I made mine. I should have taken up commercial art—I always had a touch for it. Or maybe music. My mother was a fine piano player and I inherited some of this from her. But I've had a good life—the Lord has been good to me. I was on three Olympic teams—in 1936, 1940 and 1948—and got to go overseas two times. Of course they had to cancel the Games in 1940 when Hitler invaded Norway, but I remember seeing him at Berlin in 1936 and even then he looked like a burglar. He and that fat guy, Goering. They'd sit up there and watch us run—yeah, I saw him every day. They awarded the Olympic games to *Cities,* not countries—so they told him not to mess around with things.

"I remember there was an uprising in Spain just before we were to leave New York, on the *Manhattan* for Hamburg and there was some talk that maybe we wouldn't go. But we moved out and got going and that's how I met Jesse Owens. He was the greatest track man I've ever seen—running, jumping, hurdling, anything. He could do it all. One day I'm sitting in my cabin—he's got the cabin next door—when he comes in to see me. I'm looking at my shoes and he says: 'Here, let me take a look at those.' They were marathon shoes. He wanted to try them on. I told him he'd better not. He could go up on deck and the ship might roll and his ankle might get turned. I looked at his feet and said: 'They're too small for you.' But he wanted to try them on anyway and—rrrrrrip!—he tore them right up the back. Luckily, I had three pairs with me. 'See,' I said, 'what did I tell you?' I took the shoes down to the bottom of the boat, where this Swede was, and he sewed them up for me. I gave him fifty cents. Actually, the shoes only cost seven-fifty in those days and they were beautiful. Tailor-made.

"I was the only American to finish in Berlin. But, God, it was tough. Thirteen miles out, thirteen miles back. I remember seeing Tarzan Brown along the way. He was leaning against a tree with some German soldiers. He saw me coming and said, 'Too tough, too tough.' Thank goodness I could finish. They had a rule we were supposed to get off the field the minute we finished our event. But I was so tired I just fell down on the grass. These two soldiers—big guys—came along and picked me up under the arms and started taking me out. They were only doing what they were supposed to be doing. I had no argument with them. But I kept saying, 'Hey, put me down, put me down!' They were pulling my arms out of my sockets.

"At London, I was the second American to finish. I came in twenty-first and I remember going over on the boat. There's this broadcaster down in New York, a runner himself, Marty Glickman, when he heard I was on the boat he thought it was my son. He couldn't get over that fact it was me. I was forty-two years old at the time.

77

"I ran my first Boston in 1928. I don't know if I had a job then or if I was bumming around. It's so long ago. But I was just a kid —twenty-one—and what did I know? I Vaselined up my feet and I ran right with the leaders until we got to Wellesley. Then my feet started to blister from all the Vaseline—I was wearing wool socks —and they became all bloody. I had to drop out after seventeen miles and, like I say, what did I know? Now I wear cotton socks. Cotton, not wool. I wear a size smaller, so they fit snugly, and I turn them inside out so the seam doesn't rub against my foot. Now I don't run fast enough to get blisters.

"The crowd always amazes me. Like this year. It was ninety-two degrees and they were out all along the way with their hoses and their buckets and their sponges. It was enough to make you cry. I remember I used to talk to Clarence—Clarence H. DeMar. He told me he appreciated it more at the end even when he wasn't winning. He'd tell me he'd get tears, too. You just can't help it out there. The people are all so beautiful. I think I know why they like me. I'm local. That's number one. And it's my age. People can identify with me—people in their forties, fifties and sixties. And I'm Irish, and why kid about it: Boston is primarily an Irish city.

"I remember running in Philadelphia, in a marathon they had down there. John Kelly—Grace Kelly's father—he put it on. He tried to bring some prestige to his city. I guess he must have spent three thousand dollars putting on the race. But it wasn't the same. Not like Boston. Boston has the color. Nothing can match it.

"I failed to finish only three times—that first year when I dropped out with those blisters. I said, 'Hey, this isn't for me.' I wasn't ready for anything like that. I didn't run again for four years. Then I failed to finish in 1956. I was sick and I had a sore leg. I had a lot of trouble. I had the flu, plus the leg, and I ran about nineteen or twenty miles and finally said, 'The hell with it.' A police cruiser picked me up—this was in Brookline—and they turned me over to another cruiser—this one from Boston. They took me in to the finish line. Then, in 1968, I had this hernia operation. It was March 13 and I was in the hospital for a week. The doctor wanted me to start—run just three or four miles to keep my record going. I told him, 'No way,' my health was too important.

"The most amazing year was 1945. I couldn't believe it. I couldn't believe I could feel so good. I went out and ran seventeen or eighteen miles on a Sunday and I felt terrific. I never felt that way before. I

78

came in and told my wife, 'If I feel this way in Boston, nobody is going to beat me.' And nobody did. It was one of those once-in-a-lifetime things.

"I love to run. This is just part of my life. It's the way I live. You put in so much effort and the rewards are so little, you might as well enjoy it and make a lot of friends."

10

Monsieur Cote, the Fabulous Frenchman

NEXT TO CLARENCE H. DEMAR, nobody had more success in the Boston Marathon than Gerard Cote, the happy-go-lucky Frenchman from the small town of St. Hyacinthe, near Montreal. Nobody had more fun either. It was nothing for Cote to run 26 miles 385 yards in the afternoon and dance until two o'clock in the morning. Cote won in 1940, '43, '44 and '48, and they still talk of his charm as much as his ability.

After finishing on top in 1948, Cote told the reporters gathered around him: "Gentlemens! Gentlemens! One beer! One ceegar! Then we talk about the race, eh?"

One year Cote nearly knocked Jerry Nason over in the post-race interview by saying: "I think I'll run back to Hopkinton,"

"You can't do that," said Nason.

"Why not?" asked Cote.

"Well . . . it just . . . it just isn't done," said the flabbergasted Nason.

How would that make the old race look? Nobody ever runs the course twice in the same day—much less frontward and then backward.

Cote was only kidding, of course, but he probably could have done it. He was one of the truly great athletes to compete in Boston. He was superbly conditioned from years as a snowshoe racer. Once you've gone ten miles over the snow, low to the ground, slogging along in the dead of winter, with heavy clothes on and the pain in your back burning like a hot coal—what could a few more miles over the New England countryside possibly do to a man?

Cote was a very serious runner as well as a lighthearted one. When he asked for a beer, he did it because he felt this was the best thing to drink after a race. His longtime coach, Pete Gavuzzi, taught him that. "If I drink water, I want more water," said Cote. "Pretty soon if I drink enough water, then I do not want to eat. It's better to have one beer—maybe two beers—and then you'll still have your appetite."

And the cigars?

"Those I just enjoy," said Cote.

The little man is now sixty-three years old. He still lives in St. Hyacinthe. And he still runs. Cote works in the advertising department of *Imprimerie Le Courrier*, a French-language newspaper, and after work he runs five miles a day.

"Oh, yes, I still enjoy it," he said. "It keeps the body clean. It keeps you feeling fresh. There is still nothing in the world like running."

Now that's quite a statement for any Frenchman to make, even one who is sixty-three.

But let's keep Monsieur Cote, the Fabulous Frenchman, in the proper perspective. He liked a few beers but that was all. He liked a few cigars but that was all. And when he celebrated by dancing until two o'clock in the morning, he did it with his wife.

Cote always was a dashing sort of fellow, with flashing eyes and jet-black hair as dark as a raven's wing. Like all good marathoners, he excelled at the sport only through great determination and personal sacrifice.

As a young man, he was earning only a few dollars a week as an agent for newspapers and other publications around St. Hyacinthe and Montreal. He had no club backing of any kind. His only sponsor was his father and his father was the head of a household that included eleven children. So when Cote showed up in Boston in 1940 for his sixth try, he had only $17 in his pocket. It didn't matter. He was accustomed to existing on pennies. He did the cooking for his family back home, since his mother had died, and he ironed his brothers' clothes. For a fee, naturally. Gerard Cote was a self-sufficient young man.

Even though he had no trainer and ran on his own experience and intuition, he not only won the Boston Marathon in 1940, but he broke Tarzan Brown's record in the bargain. He also broke old Johnny Kelley's heart, beating him to the line in what would be the first in a series of frustrating races for Kelley. Three times Kelley would finish second to Cote, once by only fifty seconds. Kelley had the speed, but Cote had the endurance. The Frenchman could run all day. He trained by going thirty to thirty-five miles a day. The hills of Newton never troubled him. He ran in and out of them as if he were on roller skates. Kelley was a front-runner, but Cote had him so psyched out with his amazing stamina that old Johnny tried to run from behind in 1944. It was the first time in his life he had ever tried such a tactic. But even that didn't work. Cote was too much going down to the wire. "He had the heart of a lion," Kelley would say after one of his defeats. Old Johnny wept after another, saying, "What can I do to beat him?"

Cote had a strong handle on himself. While he knew the joy of victory, he also knew the despair of defeat. And so he empathized with Kelley, saying how sorry he felt for "John-nee." "He is a great competitor," Cote would say. He kept on beating him, though.

Cote became a runner quite by accident. He was primarily interested in boxing. He read of the exploits of Joe Louis and Henry Armstrong and wanted to become a fighter himself. He knew it was a difficult profession. He knew that to be a good fighter, he would have to be in the very best of condition. That meant lots of road work—running, running and more running. That's how he got started, trotting through the picturesque streets of St. Hyacinthe, dreaming of the moment when he would climb through the ropes in Madison Square Garden and hear the ring announcer call out his name: "And from St. Hyacinthe, Quebec, weighing 130 pounds . . ."

A strange thing started happening to Cote. The more he ran, the more he liked it. The more he liked it, the less he thought about boxing. "Here," he thought to himself on one of his jaunts along the star-swept roads outside St. Hyacinthe, "is a finer sport than boxing."

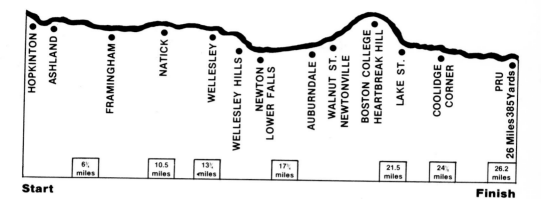

The present Boston Marathon route.

The start of the Marathon at Hayden Rowe in Hopkinton. (*Boston Globe* Photo)

The line of runners stretches out, like a giant serpent, through the New England countryside. (*Boston Globe* Photo)

Even five minutes after the start the field is still bunched. (*Boston Globe* Photo)

Not all runners wear an official number. If we don't make it to Boston, baby, we can always stop off at Wellesley and talk to the girls. (*Boston Globe* Photo)

On and on they go . . . through country roads and city streets . . . getting encouragement from the spectators along the way. (*Boston Globe* Photo)

After about an hour or two the ecstasy starts turning into agony. (*Boston Globe* Photo)

Erich Segal, the man in the middle, in happier days—when he was merely No. 667 and another plodder along the Boston trail. (*Boston Globe* Photo)

Jack Fultz, the 1976 winner, tries to beat the record 90-plus temperatures with a shower-on-the-run. (*Boston Globe* Photo)

Run for the hoses. That's just about what they did as temperatures soared during the 1976 race. (*Boston Globe* Photo)

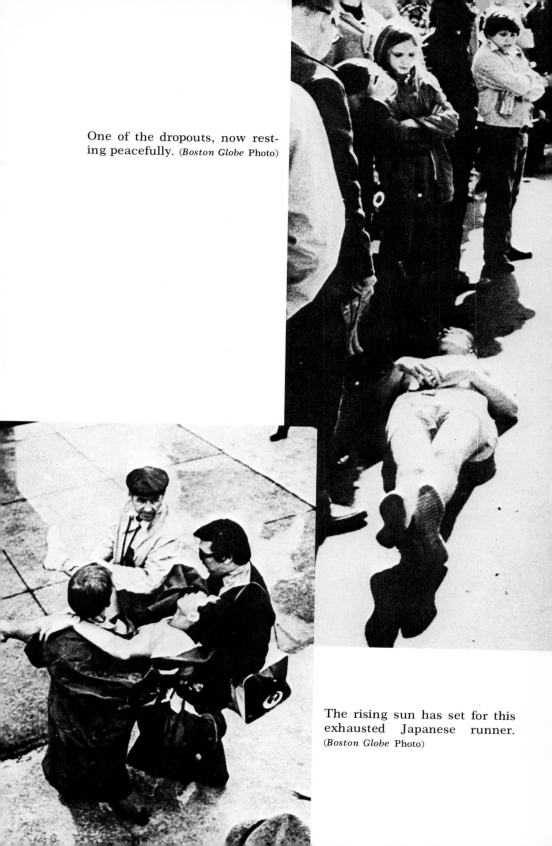

One of the dropouts, now resting peacefully. (*Boston Globe* Photo)

The rising sun has set for this exhausted Japanese runner. (*Boston Globe* Photo)

Coming into the homestretch,
oblivious of the rain but not the
pain. (*Boston Globe* Photo)

Finishers all, winners all.
(*Boston Globe* Photo)

They've run 26 miles 355 yards . . . and now they're going to put on a sprint race for the last 30 yards. (*Boston Globe* Photo)

This is what it looks like to finish a Boston Marathon. To some it looks like heaven. (*Boston Globe* Photo)

All hail the champion! He came, he saw, he conquered—the ultimate triumph. (*Boston Globe* Photo)

And here come some more winners (finishers) in the Marathon.
(*Boston Globe* Photo)

Friends to the end. Jerry Coyle (*left*) and Bob Keiss can hardly hide their elation after finishing the Boston Marathon one more time. (Photo by Rick Levy)

This is what running 26 miles can do to your feet. (*Boston Globe* Photo)

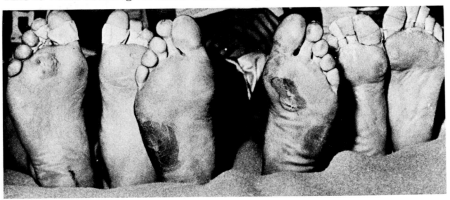

B. A. A. ROAD RACE.

ASHLAND
START ON
PLEASANT ST.
FOUNTAIN ST.
MANN ST. WINTER ST.
WEST CENTRAL ST.
SOUTH MAIN ST.
SOUTH FRAMINGHAM
GREEN ST.
LONG POND
COTTAGE ST.
NATICK
CENTRAL ST.
GROVE ST.
EAST CENTRAL ST.
WELLESLEY STA
GLEN ROAD
WASHINGTON ST.
NEWTON LOWER FALLS
SIGNBOARDS
NEWTON CENTRE
BOULEVARD
RESERVOIR
BEACON ST.
COMMONWEALTH AVE
FINISH
IRVINGTON OVAL EXETER ST.
BOSTON

ROUTE OF TODAY'S MARATHON 25 MILE
ROAD RACE

The *Boston Globe* of April 19, 1897, carried a map of the first Marathon route, which was only 24½ miles long.

INCIDENTS OF THE MARATHON ROAD RACE.

THE START

A SPURT

THE AMBULANCE CORPS

A STRAGLER

JOHN J. McDERMOTT
FINISHES AHEAD

Next day's *Boston Globe* gave highlights of the race. John J. McDermott of New York City won it in 2 hours 55 minutes 10 seconds.

The mighty Clarence H. DeMar finishing in front of the Lenox Hotel for one of his seven Boston Marathon victories. (*Boston Globe* Photo)

Ellison M. Brown, the great "Tarzan" Brown, about to cross the finish line in the rain for his second Marathon victory in 1939. (Creative Photographers, Inc., Boston)

Here comes Gerard Cote, the fabulous Frenchman, on the way to the first of his four titles in 1940.

In the most stirring of all Marathon victories, Stylianos Kyriakides, an emaciated Greek, had entered the race in 1946 in hopes of dramatizing the shortage of food afflicting his people. (*Boston Globe Photo*)

A royal escort—well, almost—leads Yoshiaki Unetani of Japan to the finish line in his 1969 triumph. (*Boston Globe* Photo)

Gene Roberts, ex-G.I., who lost both legs in Vietnam, finishes his memorable "run" in 1970. (*Boston Globe* Photo)

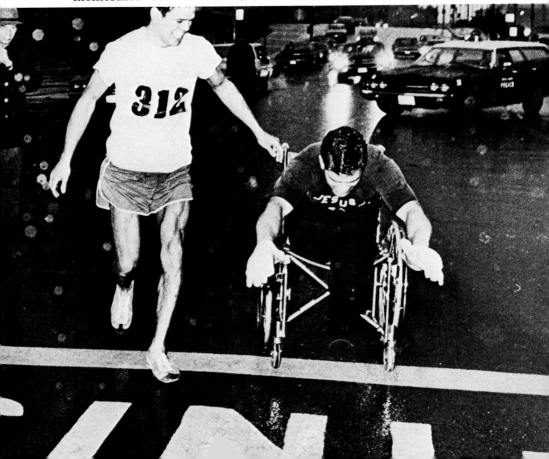

So a runner he would be. No money in it, of course. But he never had any money anyway.

Cote was adept at many sports. He was a shortstop in baseball and a pitcher in softball. He played hockey and got into the snow-shoe races in winter. He once skated in a roller derby, and won it. But running was closest to his heart.

He read about all of the great runners of the past—Paavo Nurmi, Arthur Newton and Clarence H. DeMar. He applied their techniques to his own style. When Gavuzzi became his coach, Cote learned to run great distances—greater distances than the races themselves. It was only logical, said Gavuzzi, that if you can go thirty-five miles, you should be able to go twenty-six miles, and throw in those 385 yards for good measure. It was sound advice for Cote. He became almost a machine when he ran—going on and on and on without stopping. Endurance, not speed, is what Gavuzzi believed to be the secret of marathoning. He would tell Cote, "Three hours slow is better than two hours fast." Whenever the reporters would ask Cote for his secret to running, he would tell them: "Three hours slow is better than two hours fast."

Cote also learned to accept defeat with victory and this helped to drive him to even greater heights than he might otherwise have achieved.

Speaking to a banquet in Montreal following his 1940 triumph in Boston, Cote said: "If I am beaten next time I run, do not mind. We must mix victory with defeat. If you have a salad that is all lettuce, it is not good. It has no flavor. It is flat. So victory, always, would be flat. You must mix in defeat to gain the flavor."

Cote's first victory—while very delectable—was not easily attained. He had run five times in Boston before finally reaching the top. Before the 1940 race little Gerard did his training in the streets of Montreal. That's because they kept the streets clear of snow for the motorcar traffic. Training along Notre Dame Street, Cote logged sixty to seventy miles a week—until he felt his body was ready for the test at Boston.

He took the bus to Boston by himself and luckily fell in with Walter E. Seaver, manager of the Lenox Hotel. Seaver took an immediate liking to the carefree, yet serious, Frenchman, and housed him and fed him during his stay in Boston. To this day Cote talks with deep feeling about the man who helped him through those difficult days.

At the start of the 1940 race, Kelley showed up at the starting line with a short haircut. The other runners began kidding him about it.

"Aw, I had it cut this way so the laurel wreath would fit better," said Kelley. He almost got to wear it, too, until Cote came out of nowhere to stun everyone—the runners, the press, the mobs along the way. He was considered a good runner, but a champion? Not quite.

It looked as if it would be a two-man duel between Kelley and Scotty Rankin of Preston, Ontario. That's the way it was as they headed into the long, straight run down Beacon Street. When Rankin faltered and fell back, Kelley thought the race was his.

But—clip, clop, clip, clop—here came the snowshoe runner after him, slowly cutting into Kelley's two-hundred-yard lead, pulling abreast of him and then slowly edging away. It was to be a typical Cote effort—deadly serious but also time for a wave and a kiss (actually a lot of kisses) for the crowd along the way.

"Cote's finish was a remarkable bit of running," said Kelley, whose second-place finish earned him a spot on the U.S. Olympic team. "I thought I had it won when he came up out of nowhere. He was flying. I just couldn't hold him."

Cote himself did not expect to win. He was far back at the halfway point—just another face in the crowd.

"No, I did not think it would be my day, But once I got going, I felt pretty well. Was I happy? I felt wonderrrrrrful!"

Everyone figured this would be Cote's last visit to Boston, perhaps forever since he was entering the service in Canada. But he would be back in 1943, 1944 and 1948—to beat Kelley two more times.

Cote himself didn't think he'd make it in 1943. He still ran while in the army but injured his Achilles' tendon a week before the race. From the moment the gun sounded in Hopkinton, Cote and Kelley hooked up in a tight duel. They ran in this unrelenting manner for the first twenty-one miles. Kelley tried to hang on through the tortuous climb through the hills but slowly fell back. Cote, a sergeant in the Canadian Army, pulled away and won handily. He kept looking for the "soft" spots in the road to avoid stepping in them and aggravating his leg. Still, his leg ached badly through the final mile. But the nights he had spent under a heat lamp had gotten him through.

Kelley was crushed by this defeat. His second-place finishes were beginning to gnaw at him. When he came back in 1944, he followed the advice of Leslie Pawson and laid off the pace. It was Kelley's habit to go out fast and try to burn off the competition. This time he hung back, hoping he would have enough left to catch Cote at the end. The ploy almost worked—but not quite.

Cote was confused by Kelley's strategy. He kept looking around for him but couldn't find him. Kelley finally caught up and the pair ran side by side for three miles in one of the most dramatic duels ever staged in the old race. The outcome was decided at Massachusetts and Commonwealth where Cote uncorked a sudden burst and gained a five-yard lead. Try as he would, Kelley couldn't close the gap. Cote then took off like a Thoroughbred until he added another forty yards. The two leaders were so far ahead of the field that Kelley finished nearly six minutes ahead of the next runner.

Kelley was a picture of dejection as he crossed the finish line. "Bridesmaid," he kept mumbling to himself. "Always a bridesmaid."

Kelley would win in 1945 but Cote was back to score perhaps his greatest victory, certainly the most controversial, in 1948. He won by only forty-four seconds over Ted Vogel, who was representing the B.A.A., and those who were there to see it say that the runners almost came to blows during the race.

Vogel charged Cote with all sorts of unfair tactics. "Early in the race, he stepped on my heels three or four times," Vogel stormed. "Later, when we were fighting for the lead near Lake Street, he cut in front of me time after time, breaking stride. Finally, he threw water over his head—throwing it hard enough to splash my legs and tighten them up. I don't say it was intentional but I didn't like it and I told him so."

Vogel told Cote if he threw water on him again they were going to square off right in the street. Cote merely shrugged and kept on running. Later, Cote denied any hanky-panky on his part.

"I bumped him, yes, but it was an accident," said Cote. "And I did not intentionally throw water on him. I'm sure he got some, but it was not done on purpose.

"If anything, I was hoping Vogel would win. He is young and fast. During the race I told him he was going to win. It was at the bottom of the first big hill. 'You're going to win,' I told him. 'But be careful. Tom Crane will be coming soon.' "

Tom Crane never showed and Cote turned on the power until

Vogel began to fade and finally came across the line on macaroni legs.

If they ever have a Hall of Fame for the Boston Marathon— Gerard Cote's plaque will occupy a position of honor: 1940, '43, '44 and '48.

11
Will Rodgers:
Age of Innocence

THE THREE MOST intimidating sports figures in my time have been Vince Lombardi, Ted Williams and Mickey Mantle, just about in that order.

None of us working a daily beat on football ever really interviewed Lombardi. We stood back, in awe, and asked our questions and hoped he wouldn't come down too hard on us: "What the hell kind of stupid thing is that to ask!" Lombardi had his favorites, to be sure. Arthur Daley of *The New York Times*. Tex Maule of *Sports Illustrated*. But if you were working the trenches on Sunday afternoons, Lombardi didn't notice you and didn't care if you came around. He'd keep us waiting in the hall outside the Green Bay dressing room as long as his mood dictated. Nobody complained. Who were you going to complain to? Pete Rozelle? He wasn't going to do anything about it. He stood in awe of the man himself—the man who meant so much to professional football in those growing years of the 1960s.

Williams? I was lucky. I was a Detroit writer and when he began his great feud with the Boston press, Williams always said give him someone like the writers from Detroit. *They* understood the game, which meant they understood him. It was a ruse, of course—Williams' way of letting the world know that he could get along with writers, and he picked Detroit since we had some of the easiest-going men in the league covering baseball.

As for the Mick, it was always difficult to talk to him because the Yankees were rollicking around the country in those days doing pretty much as they wanted—on and off the field. One of the favorite games in the Yankee clubhouse was "Embarrass the Writers." You'd ask a question and maybe somebody like Clete Boyer would make a smart remark and everybody would start laughing. It was tough standing there trying to keep your dignity but knowing it was slowly slipping away. Mantle was a player of such ability, such stature, that this alone made it difficult to interview him. On the days when things didn't go well with him—as when Frank Lary was pitching for the Tigers—you'd stand there hoping he would look up so you could ask the first question. Sometimes you had to ask it when he didn't look up. Sometimes he didn't even answer you.

So now here is Will Rodgers and he is sitting in a booth at the Eliot Lounge on a Sunday night and it's hard to get the interview going because what is he but the kid next door. He is every bit as much a giant as Williams or Mantle or Lombardi, but you would never guess it. He has run the fastest Boston Marathon in history, the fastest in the eighty years of this event. The day was right for him, cool with a strong breeze at his back. But others have had these conditions and nobody ever ran from Hopkinton to Boston the way Will Rodgers did in 1975: 2:09.55. He ran with white gloves which he ultimately removed, a white headband, which also came off, and a ragtag jersey with the words "Boston GBTC" on the front.

It was was such an incredible feat and yet such an easy story to write:

By Joe Falls
Free Press Sports Editor

BOSTON—Young Will Rodgers stopped for a drink. Thank you, ma'am.

Then he stopped again and took another Dixie Cup filled with water. Thank you, sir.

And, finally, most incredible of all, he stopped and tied his shoelace.

Such was the legend of this 79th running of the Boston Marathon; how this lean, lithe young man stopped no fewer than three times and still ran the greatest race in the history of this ancient classic.

Rodgers took on the largest field the Boston race has ever known, doctors, lawyers and Indian chiefs numbering a colossal 2,041, and swept through the New England countryside like no man since Paul Revere 200 years ago.

Of course, I had my facts wrong. Rodgers stopped five times, not three, during his record-breaking run. Four times for water, once for his shoelace.

I remember asking him in the madhouse of the press conference in the Pru, "Why did you *stop* to drink?"

"Gee," he said, "I just can't hold the cup while I'm running."

Never thought of that.

But this is Will Rodgers—a pure, plain, simple, honest, innocent young man. He never dreamed he would be running the race that once favored the likes of Clarence H. DeMar, the two John Kelleys, Gerard Cote, Leslie Pawson, Ron Hill, and all of those fleet Finns and Japanese and even that Colombian—what's his name? Alvaro Mejia, who won by only five seconds over Pat McMahon in the closest race in Boston's history and then jumped into the water fountain because his feet were burning up from blisters. Young Will actually quit racing five years before his great Boston triumph. His roommate, Amby Burfoot, the winner of the 1968 Boston Marathon, tried to talk him into coming back and taking up road racing.

"I hated it," Rodgers said. "It was too hot. Too tiring. I dropped running after an 8:58 two-mile—quit, just like that. I began smoking half a pack of cigarettes a day and when I moved to Boston and got a job at Peter Bent Brigham Hospital, I got myself a motorcycle for transportation."

Then two things happened.

Somebody stole his motorcycle, so he had to run to work, and he began fooling around at the Y.M.C.A. track. When a guy of about sixty beat him in a race, Rodgers gave up his cigarettes and got serious about this business of running.

And so here he is, one of the world's class marathon runners, in T-shirt and jeans, sitting in a booth at the Eliot Lounge and if you care for a little innocence—no Lombardian scowls, Williams-like glares or Mantle-like contempt—you may listen in:

Question: What's it mean to be the Boston Marathon record holder?

Answer: It's brought me a tremendous amount of attention. Media attention, a chance to run in a lot of races, free equipment —a lot of travel expense money, which I was never able to get before.

Q: Who provides expense money?

A: Race sponsors, institutions in the form of businesses, newspapers and even individual businessmen.

Q: Where have you been since winning at Boston?

A: I've been to Holland, Japan twice and Puerto Rico. My first trip was to Puerto Rico where I won and then I went to Holland where I lost. I dropped out. I went over and back in two days and the jet-lag got to me.

Q: And Japan?

A: The first time the Japanese Athletic Association paid for it. This was for the World Championship in the marathon. I finished third. The second time I went I was sponsored by a Japanese newspaper, which has an agreement with the Boston A.A. for the first two finishers to go over there and run in the Japanese races. The second time I was there they had eight thousand starters.

Q: Eight thousand?

A: It wasn't much different than Boston. It didn't seem like that to me . . . I guess we were up front and got out ahead of them. It was on an out-and-back course and on the way back we could see a lot of runners going the other way. We waved to them and they waved back at us. I guess it was something at that—two Americans and the rest were Japanese. The other American was Tom Fleming of New Jersey and we did have a good time, cheering and waving back and forth.

Q: Have your friends treated you any differently now that you're a champion, a celebrity, really?

A: No, not really. Runners are sort of a hang-loose independent group of people. Oh, I've had a few good times out of winning the Marathon and maybe some people will ask me for my autograph. But it's nothing special. You may have a fast time, as I did, but you realize you can only run well for a certain amount of time. Everyone is vulnerable and I know I am, too. My record will go— and that'll be good. I like to see records broken, even if they're my own. That's what running is all about.

Q: How could you stop five times and still set a record?

A: I don't know. I didn't stop long—maybe five seconds and

swooooosh! I was off again. I even stop when I'm training. It's just a natural thing for me to do.

Q: You seem to run with such an even pace all the way, like you had no trouble at all keeping up with the press bus?

A: It's true . . . your best times come in an even-paced race. I was lucky that day. It was a good day to run and I was psyched up and I had good competition. I didn't go out real fast and didn't finish up real fast. The middle of the race was the strongest part of my race.

Q: Why is the Boston Marathon considered the greatest race of all?

A: It's old. It's the oldest marathon . . . and . . . well, other than that I don't know why it's considered the greatest.

Q: You got married eight months after winning in Boston. Has that affected your running in any way?

A: Yes, my wife, Ellen, has helped me out a lot. I don't spend so much time now sitting around in bars drinking beer. She encourages me to run. That's important. Some wives, or girl friends, never encourage their men. I don't know why, but they don't.

Q: Is running a joy to you?

A: Sometimes. Sometimes it's an incredible drag. Just yesterday I went out and ran about twenty-three miles and I was swearing at people and hitting mailboxes. I didn't want to be out there but I knew I had to. I'd say most runners half-like and half-dislike running.

Q: How do you combat boredom out there?

A: I like to look at things when I run, so I just try to find interesting places to run.

Q: How much do you run each week?

A: I run between one hundred and one hundred and sixty miles.

Q: Has running made you a better person?

A: No. It hasn't made me more moral, if that's what you mean. It's made me happier, though. Every time I finish a workout, I feel good. If I work out twice a day, I feel twice as good.

Q: I never thought of that. How long would you like to run?

A: Until I'm dead.

91

12

"Ladies, Start Your Engines!"

THE BIG GREYHOUND ROLLED TO A STOP at the bus depot in downtown Boston and look who got off: Joan of Arc.

Nope, she didn't arrive from La Belle France, merely from San Diego, four days, four nights, nonstop, sleeping fitfully in her cramped seat, eating erratically, carrying a bag and a pair of new running shoes.

History was about to be made, even if Jock Semple and Will Cloney, the guardians of the proud Boston Marathon, didn't know it.

In fact, Roberta Gibb didn't know it. She knew they didn't like women running in their race, but she had no idea—no notion whatever—that she would be the first female to traverse the 26 miles 385 yards from Hopkinton to Boston.

Still, she wasn't taking any chances. Her mom, who lived in Winchester, Massachusetts, drove her out to Hopkinton the next morning, where Roberta concealed herself in a thicket. She slipped out and joined the pack when half the men had passed her point of concealment.

The curious thing is that she ran the entire distance—stride for stride with the guys—and nobody noticed her. All she was wearing was an ensemble of black leotards and a beret. Why would anyone think that was unusual? The date was April 19, 1966. It would be six more years before the ladies would be allowed to run officially, but here was pretty Roberta—and she was a stunning gal of twenty-three, slim and trim, smooth of stride and smooth of skin—who whirled home in three and a half hours. They didn't have the clock on her because nobody even knew she was out there. "What girl?" Cloney was to say later in the evening. "I know of no woman who ran. Our rules do not permit women to run."

But run it she did, and while it was Katherine Switzer—the immortal K. Switzer—who got in on an official-unofficial basis the following year by getting a number from the old B.A.A. and causing that classic shoving match involving the inimitable Jock Semple, it was Roberta Louise Gibb who is the matron saint of the Boston Marathon. She was the one who blazed the way for the gals to get in on the big run to Boston. It became official on March 28, 1972, when Cloney harrumphed a couple of times and told the world that a tradition of seventy-five years was going by the boards: The ladies could compete just like gentlemen. All they had to do was qualify, just like the guys.

Cloney said they would be given every courtesy extended to the men—their own dressing quarters at the First Congregational Church in Hopkinton and also at the end of the race in the Prudential Building in downtown Boston. They'd even have a couple of lady doctors to look at their bunions. In other words, on March 28, 1972, the women of the world were looked upon as first-class citizens by the Boston Athletic Association. It was a mere fifty-two years after they had been accorded the right to vote.

Nobody believed a gal could go the whole distance. The cynics—and they were a legion—believed that Roberta probably had jumped out of the bushes in Wellesley or maybe slipped into line somewhere along Commonwealth Avenue. Everybody was talking about it. Did she or didn't she? That night, in one of the strong male bastions of Boston—the locker room of the Boston Celtics—the debate raged at great length. The Celtics were merely engaged in a game against the Los Angeles Lakers, featuring Jerry West and Elgin Baylor, but the topic was girls or, more accurately, lady runners.

One of the Boston writers, pouring fuel on the flames of debate, even got her name wrong. He called her Roberta Bingay. No matter. She was still a gal and had she or hadn't she?

Earl Wilson, the Red Sox pitcher who was visiting before the game, said: "I ran two miles once and I nearly collapsed. No girl ever ran a Marathon. Never."

Red Auerbach, the general manager of the Celts, shook his head in puzzlement. "It's hard to believe," he said. "I can't get these guys to run around the floor and a small broad goes out there and runs a Marathon. I don't know what this world is coming to."

One of the Celtic players—who shall have to remain nameless—shook his head in wonderment (which is almost the same as puzzlement).

"If there's a goer in this town like that, how come I don't know her?" he said.

Not even Lady Godiva created this sort of stir among the male populace, and as the years passed, the truth came out simply because there was no reason any more to hide it. Roberta did run, and run well, and the last of the Boston barriers began to cave in.

Jock Semple was not ready to yield—not yet. Whenever Roberta Gibb's name came up, the veins in his neck would pop. "The hell she ran," he fumed. "And I'll tell ye this—they don't belong in races where they don't belong and I 'kin not get any more logical than that. An' if any try to get in, they're gonna get thrown out."

At least Jock was true to his word. When K. Switzer—who turned out to be 20-year-old Katherine Switzer, a coed from Syracuse University—showed up the next year wearing No. 261, Jock jumped from the press bus and tried to tear the numbers from her sweat shirt. The cameras were grinding, since the photo truck happened to be right on the scene, and photos of Jock pushing Kathy and Kathy's boyfriend pushing Jock went around the world and appeared in thousands of newspapers.

Jock came off looking like the Boston Strangler.

Kathy Switzer got in when her entry blank carried only her first initial: K. That could be Kurt. Or Karl. Or King Kong. Nobody dreamed it would mean Kathy, or Katherine.

Kathy says she wrote down her initial—K.—simply because that's how she signed everything, her checks, her bills, her school papers, everything. She claims—and nobody believes her to this day, not even her boyfriend—that she was innocent of any hanky-panky. She claims she simply wanted to run in Boston and that's all there was to it.

Yet, she remained in the car (it was drizzling) while her coach went into the gym in Hopkinton to pick up her number. And (it was still drizzling) she kept her hood on until the race was under way. The evidence can be read either way, though Kathy insists she was not trying to put one over on the guys. She knew she wouldn't be welcomed, but she felt she had met all the qualifications to run and that's what she wanted to do. Why start combing your hair at the starting line if it'll create a fuss?

Now the barrier that had started to wobble with Roberta Gibb's first appearance began to crumble over l'Affaire Switzer. Many of the writers—notably Bud Collins of the *Boston Globe*—took up the cause of the ladies and chided the old B.A.A. for keeping the gals out. Bud said, for heaven's sake, didn't they know this was 1967, supposedly an era of enlightenment. So chivalry was dead, said Bud; did it have to be replaced by boorishness? Jock Semple kept that article in his desk drawer and would take it out on occasion and turn purple every time he read it. Eight months later, he took the column out and tore it to shreds.

Jerry Nason, the Boswell of Boston, first looked on with interest, then took up the sword for the ladies. He remembered a report that there was a woman on the course as far back as 1951—a "lady in red"—but not much fuss was made of it since she made no appearance at the finish line. Jerry first became fascinated by the ladies when he saw Fanny Blankers Koen, the great Dutch runner, the marvelous mother of three, win four gold medals at the London Olympics in 1948.

"She sold me on what women could do," Nason said. "She showed me that men didn't have any monopoly on enthusiasism. And this wasn't any heavy-muscled giant either. This was a lady, a Venus, and my God, how she could run!"

So the old race, creaking along for years, was undergoing a major upheaval. Roberta Gibb was back in 1968 and she became a genuine heroine. As she whizzed down the hill at Prudential Center, an official announced: "And running up is an unofficial entry, Roberta Gibb of Winchester." The mobs roared. Roberta kept right on running, past the finish line, past the photographers, past the waiting reporters—right into the Pru's underground garage. She was unable to catch her breath. Her father told reporters: "She finished too strong—she has to slow down gradually to get her heart adjusted." Marathon officials (maybe not the ogres they were being portrayed as) had a private locker room waiting for Roberta, but she chose to dress in the ladies' room in the garage.

And then, more women came across the finish line. Mrs. Majorie Fish, a 36-year-old Cambridge mother of four, was the second. She said she had hidden behind a telephone pole before the start to get in the race without being noticed. Mrs. Fish ran with her husband, Howard MacFarland Fish, Jr., a minister at Harvard, and no one—not even Jock Semple—was about to hassle with the clergy.

Remembering the stir created by The Great Shoving Scandal of 1967, the ladies were still wary of running. Miss Gibb's father dropped his daughter out of the car "in a patch of woods about one hundred yards from the starting line." Miss Gibb had also been a member of the 1967 race, but nobody noticed her because of the furor over Miss Switzer. This time Miss Gibb sidled up to the starting line and once she got started, she had no problems. Even the police along the way cheered her on.

Kathy Switzer remained out of the 1968 race. Her ex-boyfriend was trying to win a place on the U.S. Olympic team as a hammer thrower, and he felt any more adverse publicity wouldn't do anyone any good. Anyway, the A.A.U.—another stuffy organization—banned Kathy from running on every ground it could think of, including running without a chaperon. The A.A.U. never said what it thought big Tom Miller was doing out there in 1967, not to mention Arnie Briggs, her coach. Anyway, Kathy sat this one out.

In 1968 four women were recorded at the finish line, including Nina Kuscsik, who would make history of her own in 1972 when she would be accepted as the first "official" women's winner of the Boston Marathon.

Now the barrier was all the way down and a very unexpected thing happened, as least as far as Jock Semple and others like him were concerned. The ladies did not get in anyone's way, and indeed they added some spice (and everything nice) to the ancient road race. They were fun. They were bouncy, they were colorful —and some of them were excellent runners.

When Nina Kuscik—divorced and trying to beat her husband —became the first official women's winner in 1972, she celebrated by dancing until two o'clock in the morning. Kathy Switzer ran that year and it was so hot by the time they got to Framingham that she dashed into the rest room of a gas station and took off her black body-stocking, cut it down to panties and ran the rest of the way in panties and tunic. Kathy, in fact, was becoming one of the most widely interviewed lady athletes in the world— a role she loved.

Reporter: "What does long-distance running do to you?"

Kathy: "It makes me more sensuous."

What sportswriter (political writer, science writer, medical writer, etc.) wouldn't like to get that sort of answer for his story.

Kathy was good at it because she was a free spirit and the time was exactly right for free spirits. Especially female free spirits.

"When I'm training, I'm more physically sensitive to food, to weather, to touch . . . everything," she said. "I also become more mentally sensitive to social problems, the ills of the world and so on. When I'm not in training, I'm more lethargic and apathetic.

"Everything I see and feel is more extreme when I'm in training. If I'm happy, I'm happier. If I'm sad, I'm sadder. If I'm emotional, I'm more emotional. I once ran thirty-one miles and after that there was nothing in the world I thought I couldn't do."

A freshness existed about the lady runners and they provided colorful copy for the writers covering the Marathon.

When you've got a Jacqueline Hansen coming in 364th—a flying Florence Nightingale is what she was—in a field of a few thousand and then going out and celebrating on pepperoni pizza and root beer, you have yourself a story.

Jock Semple tried to stand firm.

Early in the 1969 race a small runner, topped by a head of long, curly hair, crossed the finish line. No one expected a girl to finish so soon.

"Well, I only ran about seventeen miles," said the mini-marathoner. "I started around Wellesley."

"Did you know that females are not supposed to run in this race?" said Jock.

"But I'm a boy," protested the young runner, who turned out to be Gideon Ansell of Wayland, Massachusetts.

But even old Jock—poor old Jock—finally came around and in an unguarded moment, as when opening the mail in his musty office in the Boston Garden, he would reveal his admiration for the ladies—their courage and their determination.

"At least they no lie like some of these men," he blurted out one day. "And I'll tell ye, a lot of them are'n better shape than the men. You'll not see a fat woman in my race."

Jock even kissed and made up with Kathy Switzer—actually kissed her. It came about as so many of these things do—abruptly, on the spur of the moment. He just grabbed her at the starting line and gave her a big smooch—with the cameras aimed their way.

And the ladies knew they were home when, in 1972, Jock Semple presented Kathy Switzer with a trophy for finishing in the top three women.

The trophy, unfortunately, was broken.

"He apologized to me and said if I sent it back I could have another one," Kathy recalled. "Then he sputtered out with, 'Darn, I've been mad at ye for five years and ye deserve a broken trophy.'"

Home free.

Kathy Switzer came up to my room at the Hotel Roosevelt in New York, kicked off her shoes and said: "Can you order me up a couple of beers—I'm dying of thirst. And tell 'em to put the bottles in ice. Lots of ice. I like my beer ice cold."

Katherine V. Switzer is not your ordinary woman. Not your ordinary athlete.

To this date, she is the only athlete I have ever interviewed who beat off a mugger—a rapist?—in Central Park. It happened in 1974.

She was out running in the park when, suddenly, she was grabbed from behind by a man.

"The worst part of it was that he was in a jogging suit and running right behind me," said Kathy. "Then he had his hand on my throat and a knife at my Adam's apple.

"At first he told me not to scream, that he only wanted my money. That was crazy, because people in sweat suits don't carry money."

Kathy was carrying a spray can of dog repellent. She let him have it right in the eyes. He was momentarily blinded—and she sped off to safety.

"It was a really traumatic experience," she said. "That night I packed my bags and moved out of New York. Now I do my running near my home in White Plains. I hope that beer is going to be cold."

It was an unusual interview. I asked one question: "Tell me about running, Kathy." She talked for two sides of the tape, ninety minutes, or 26 miles 385 yards:

"The reason I ran in the Boston Marathon is that it was the last open competition—the last bastion of everyone competing together. That's the beauty of it and that's what appealed to me.

"I'd been a runner without a forum. I was a woman distance runner in an era when women weren't allowed to compete in distance races. All we could run was a mile and a half.

"I started running at nineteen and ran in my first Boston Marathon at twenty. I played all the sports at Lynchburg College in Lynchburg, Virginia, all the sports for women—field hockey, basketball and lacrosse. I was very good at field hockey. I was pretty plump then. I wore spectacles and I had big feet and I was always tripping over them. Now look at me—skinny, big hands, long arms. But I wanted very much to be good at something.

"My father said to me, 'If you want to be a good field-hockey player, you should run a mile a day.' That seemed like climbing Everest to me but every day in the summer I ran that mile. I tried out for the JV team and made first string. I started and finished every game. I thought, going to college, that all the girls would be tough—good athletes, all of them. I didn't know anything about running. I didn't know anything about training. Basically, I was feminine. Basically, I liked boys. Basically, I liked parties. Basically, I wanted to be a cheerleader but my parents thought that was very silly, and that's how I went out for sports. I ran my mile a day and an amazing thing happened when I got to school. Not only was I the best field-hockey player there, but I could outlast everybody in a game. It's funny, but the boys didn't tease me about it. Maybe if I had buck teeth or pigtails, they'd have probably kidded me a lot. They teased the other girls, but for some reason they didn't tease me. I got away with it.

"So now I figure, hey, if I run a mile and I can play this good, what would happen if I ran more. So I started adding on a quarter of a mile a week, working it up slowly, and I thought I was pretty hot stuff. I thought I was king of the hill. Nobody could run like me.

"But I was so frustrated, too. Here I was playing with these out-of-shape girls who were just messing around, having a good time. They didn't even try to play right. When I played sports, I went out for the kill. Sports were never fun to me. They were an outlet for aggression or a catharsis for all my emotions . . . or whatever you want to call it. I would always give a hundred percent when I was with these girls. They were just out there for the fun of it. It was a social thing with them. To me it was all out. Here I thought I was in terrible shape and I'm the best player on the team. Even in my second year, as a sophomore, they made me captain of the team.

"But I was so frustrated. I went into basketball, but I wasn't very good. I'm left-handed and I could never shoot. But I was a great guard and a fantastic runner. In those years they were just letting the girls go across the middle line and move around and so I was always the roving player. I could run like hell. I could never get enough of my aggression out in practice, and so when we were done, I'd run around the gym a million times. They'd look at me and wonder what I was trying to do. I had trouble with the girls and with the coaches. They couldn't understand why I'd stay out and work so long.

"Then I got into lacrosse and it was glorious. When we played field hockey and I passed to someone and they missed the goal, I would be crushed. I'd just about want to die. I'd look at them and say, 'How could you miss it—it was a perfect play?' I'd be crushed. Lacrosse was beautiful, because if you got the ball and you weren't willing to pass it off, you could cradle it all the way down the field and shoot it yourself. It was a very individualistic sport, and it was then that I knew how great it was to be a runner. I'd take off and feel like a fleet-footed Indian just flying through the woods. I felt—I had the ball and nobody can catch me. It was the greatest feeling in the world. For the first time in my life I knew what it was like to be the master of my own destiny.

"I practiced a lot . . . I ran all over the field . . . and while I was running I found myself being able to think clearly. What did I do right? What did I do wrong? I thought about my writing, my schoolwork—everything came so clear to me. The coach and I got into a big fight and she kicked me off the team. She'd tell me if I had enough energy to get out there and run after practice, then I wasn't putting out enough effort in practice. My contention was that her practices weren't demanding enough, and we went around and around like that for a long time. All I was trying to do was build up my own strength, and what did she care what I was doing anyway. What happened is, it all finally came to a head. I'd been pinned to a man at Annapolis and I gave up my last game to go to Annapolis for June week. Now the coach said I'd let the team down. 'My God,' I told her, 'we're unbeaten, we haven't lost a game yet, we can't lose the championship. What did this one game mean?' She said I was letting the team down and that's when she kicked me off.

"Suddenly I realized that I hated team concepts, I hated social concepts, I hated having to stand or fall on what a group did. If I was going to stand or fall, I wanted it to be on my own. If I was going to fall flat on my face, I wanted it to be my fault. But if I was going to score that goal—or cross that finish line—I wanted it to be all me. I wanted that feeling of ecstasy. I wanted to know that everything was going to be a result of *my* efforts. So it had to be something to do with running.

"I thought of tennis. Naw, you needed somebody else and you needed a tennis court. Golf? Golf moves too slowly and you need all that equipment and it takes too much time. I wanted something where I could be totally free—something where I could really relate to my environment. I wanted to run through the fields and throw up my hands and say, 'Wow! I'm alive! I'm me and I'm alive!' So I gave up everything I had and I had tons of equipment—tons of trophies, tons of letters, tons of certificates. I was the captain of all the teams, all-East Coast in field hockey, but I gave it all up just to run.

"I didn't know anything about running, except what I saw on TV. I knew somebody like Wilma Randolph was a runner, but I couldn't relate to her. She was running on a track and she was running one hundred yards and that's something I couldn't relate to at all. I couldn't relate to speed.

"A boy I was dating was on the cross-country team at school, and I saw him out at practice one day and I asked him if I could run with him. Sure. Fine. Terrific. He took off in a dead run and I took off after him. He was going to go all out, over the golf course, for three miles. My rear end—you won't know what this is like unless you are a runner—but we're running for a while and my rear end starts to hurt. It's like I've been sitting on it all day and it's starting to get numb. It goes right down the back of my legs and now I feel like I'm going to puke. If I can only keep him in my sights. He's running like mad and I'm trying to stay up with him. He finally stops—he's all bent over and he's trying to catch his breath when I come up to him. I don't believe it. I'm puffing and my rear end is hurting and I say to him, 'Does your rear end hurt when you run?' He just looks at me and shakes his head and walks away. I didn't know if I did good or bad. Later on, he told me I did quite good. That's when I made the biggest switch in my life. I decided I would be a runner.

"I liked to run through the woods, but then it was springtime and the woods were all gooey, thick with mud from the spring rains, so I couldn't go out there. So I did some time on the track, just ran some laps by myself. One day it was raining and the track coach come out and I'll never forget this scene. He had one of those hoods on and it was raining and he had a whole bunch of stopwatches in his hands, where all the strings hang down and come down through your fingers. I'm the only one out there and I can see he is starting to time me. I'm taking my time, like I must have been running a ten-minute mile, when he calls me over and says: 'Can you run a mile?' 'Are you kidding—sure I can run a mile.' He says he just lost eleven of his runners. They flunked off the team because there'd been a change in eligibility. He says he's got a track meet coming up Saturday and he needs somebody to run the mile. He says, 'We're probably going to lose anyway but if you can just finish, you can pick up some points for us.' It was kind of like he was saying, 'If I can get my dog to run and if he stays on the inside lane for four laps, we'll get some points.' But I said I'd be glad to help—anything for the school. That kind of stuff.

"Well, this was a Wednesday. The word got out that a woman was going to run on the *men's* track team. This created an incredible fuss. Now this was a tiny little southern school and the local newspaper got wind of the story. The AP bureau in Richmond picked it up and then the papers in Washington got in on it. It was quite a sensation—it was my first feeling of being under pressure—I mean on the basis of being a female.

"I ran a six-minute mile. About 6:02, as I remember it. And I finished last. But I got those points and that's all that mattered to me.

"So I kept running on the team—I was naïve then, you under-

102

stand. I wasn't paying attention to a whole lot of things. I could run in some meets, but I couldn't run in others. I just never gave it much thought. All of this is leading up to what happened in Boston and now I'm going to tell you the truth about Boston. Nobody ever believes me when I say it. Even my fiancé, the one I've been living with the past three years, he says, 'That's fine, sweetie. If you want to tell your little story go ahead and tell it. It's okay with me.' But what I'm going to tell you about Boston is the truth. I did *not* know it was against the rules for me to run in Boston.

"But anyway, back to college. Right after I ran that first race there were all kinds of opinions going around campus. You'd have thought I was the most reprehensible person in the world running with the boys. Here I was out there in shorts and a shirt and that meant I had to have a bad reputation. It must have meant I was messing around with all the boys. I couldn't believe it. I was so hurt. I was tremendously hurt. I was doing something wonderful —something that was so wonderfully right, so wonderfully healthy —what difference did it make if I was running with men or women or dogs or cats or horses. This was the first time I felt the sting of social stigma and I didn't know how to handle it.

"I'd made an agreement with my parents—if they could pick out my school for the first two years, I could pick out my school for the next two years. So I was ready to transfer. I didn't want to stick with liberal arts, so I went to Syracuse University and got into their journalism class. I jogged all that summer and when I went to Syracuse I walked into the track coach's office one day and said, 'Hi, this is me, I really want to run, I know I'm not good enough to run on the men's team, but do you mind if I work out with you?' He said 'No, not at all—you're welcome to work out with us.' This was Bob Grieve—he's dead now—but he was a good coach. He had a couple of national champions back in his heyday, but he died a very bitter man. As they do at all schools, they cut back on the minor sports to help out the football team and when they cut back on track, Bob got very bitter about it. I considered him a fair man. When I went out to work, he didn't pay any attention to me—but he didn't give me a hard time, either. He kind of ignored me. But that was okay. I was getting a little older and could understand things a little better.

"One day I'm out on the golf course, limbering up, getting ready to run with the cross-country team, when this little man—he seemed so small at the time, almost like a sparrow—he came up to me and said: 'Hi, are you going to run today?' He's got a baggy sweat suit on and he's old and gray and I say, 'Yes, I'm going to run.' He says, I'm Arnie Briggs and I'm sort of the unofficial coach around here. I'm the assistant coach and I've been working with these guys for twenty-five years.' He said he was just coming off a knee injury, so why don't we just run together. So we ran together. Every day he came out and we ran along and we became big pals.

"He was a mailman and every day when he'd get finished with his route, he'd come out and run. He'd be hobbling along and I wanted to go faster, but we'd kind of hang together. He'd start telling me what to do out there—Keep your arms out! Stretch your legs out! Concentrate on exhaling! Every day we'd run a little longer, a little better. What was happening is that I was learning to run as Arnie's leg was getting better. And he was always talking. He'd regale me with stories that I now call 'Tales of the Ancient Marathoner.' It turned out that Arnie was a marathoner. He'd run in the Boston Marathon and he'd run in places like New York and Baltimore. He told me about the time they had a race in New York City, from somewhere in the city out to LaGuardia Airport, which was new, and Mayor LaGuardia himself started the race. They measured off the course with a car and it turned out to be thirty-one miles. They ran and ran and ran into the night. They had to give flashlights to the runners. Johnny Kelley won the race in something like four hours and thirty-eight minutes and he was so mad at the end—he came in and said, 'Goddamn it to hell, What kind of race is this anyway?' He was so mad he wanted to spit.

"But this is what I was getting—we'd run and I'd listen to Arnie . . . and pretty soon we were running ten miles a day. My God, I thought, this is the greatest thing in the world. We'd be exhausted, the both of us, but we'd be so happy. We were running everywhere—over the golf course, over the hills, to another town and back. I was so filled with myself I couldn't believe it. One day we ran thirteen miles and Arnie was telling me about running in the Boston Marathon. We were out of breath and putting on our sweats and I said to him, 'Arnie, I'm going to run in the Boston Marathon.' He said, "You can't run the Boston Marathon." I said, 'I'm going to do it.' He said, 'You can't do it—a woman can't run the Boston Marathon.' Well, that year Roberta Gibb ran in Boston and he said no woman could run the Boston Marathon. He said, 'She must have started in the middle of the race.' I just said, 'Arnie, I'm going to run in it.'

Arnie didn't know me that well yet. When somebody tells me I can't do something, I'm going to do it. I said to him, 'Right now we're going to start training for it. Will you help me?'

"We started running ten to twelve miles a day, saving our big runs for the weekends. Then we'd go fifteen miles, then eighteen, finally up to twenty. Then one day we decided we were going to go the full twenty-six miles. I'll tell you, I was so psyched up, I couldn't wait for the day.

"It was one of those cold, crisp kind of days you get in the spring. It was the middle of March and we were going to start out in the morning. If it took us all day, we were going to run those twenty-six miles. Now, of course, this is silly. Nobody runs twenty-six miles to get ready for Boston. Are you kidding. Some guys go there and they've never run twenty-six miles in their life. You just don't do it. Now I run fifteen miles, hard. But what did I know then?

"Anyway, we measured out a course in a car and off we go. We're running along and it's fine. We're really doing well. I'm on some kind of high. We're talking all the way. Then the thought strikes me: What if we didn't measure it right? What if it's only twenty-four miles, instead of twenty-six? I'd just about die if it wasn't twenty-six.

"As we're getting near the end, I say to Arnie: 'Do you think you can do one more three-mile loop?' He says, 'What?' I say, 'Do you think you can do one more three-mile loop?' He says, 'I don't know.' I say, 'Let's try it.'

Now we're going along—Arnie's on my right side and I notice he's starting to drift out into the road and then drift back. A car comes by and I don't know if you know about cars. Sometimes they try to force you off the road, like they try to sideswipe you. Arnie jumped. They really didn't come that close to us but he jumps. I realize his visual perception is off, but he turns around and screams at them: 'You lousy no good sons of bitches! Get off the road!' He'd never sworn in front of me before and now he's picking up a rock and throwing it at the car. 'I'll break your Goddamned window,' he's screaming, and now this is a saint of a man. He's the sweetest man I've ever known in my life. 'Now, Arnie, take it easy,' I tell him. I kind of hook my arm under his, like helping somebody across the street, and I hold him close to me and we start running again. I'm trying to make up little jokes. 'Left foot, right foot, left foot, right foot.' Anything to get his mind off running. He's still cursing under his breath. Finally, we finish. We've gone almost thirty miles! I'm so happy I'm jumping up and down. 'We did it Arnie! We did it!' I slap him on the back—and he faints. Falls right over in my arms and faints. I lower him down on the curb and he's out cold. I can't help myself. I'm still jumping up and down I'm so happy. Arnie opens one eye and looks at me and says: 'You can run in the Boston Marathon.'

"The next day Arnie's waiting for me in the car. He's got all these papers on his lap. He pulls out one and gives it to me. 'What's that?' I say. He says, 'It's an entry form. If you're going to run in the Boston Marathon, you've got to fill out an entry form.' I say to him, 'I don't need to enter. Roberta Gibb didn't enter.' Arnie looks at me and says, 'You can't run unless you enter.' He said I couldn't get a number unless I entered. I tried to tell him I didn't need a number, but he insisted I fill out the form. 'Okay,' I said, 'but I don't think they're going to like me in Boston.'

"Arnie sat up. 'I don't give a damn if they like you or not. You're a qualified marathon runner and you can run in the marathon. Please fill out the form.'

"He sat there shaking his head.

" 'You've got to wear a number,' he said. 'Everybody wears a number.'

"I said, 'Okay, okay,' but my feeling was that I was going to be an intruder. Remember, this was at a time when women were upsetting male egos all over the place.

"Now I've always signed my name K. Switzer. I sign all my checks, all my bills, that way, and so that's how I signed my name on the entry blank. Arnie says to me to go over to the infirmary and get an exam from the doc. He laughed. 'Let him listen to your heart, He'll let you run.'

"We drove to Boston. Me, Arnie, John Leonard who was on the cross-country team, and Tom Miller, whom I was going to marry later on. Tom was a tremendous athlete. I was dating him all year. He had this fantastic coordination. He was just a beautiful athlete and here I was, just a plodder. He'd never run over thirteen miles, but if I was going to run in Boston, he was going to run in Boston. Ha, ha, ha.

"It was raining and cold the morning of the race—it was sleeting outside. We stayed in the car while Arnie went into the gym to give them our physical certificates. It was no trouble. He came out with these packets with our numbers and pins in them. About ten minutes before race time, we got out of the car and started doing warm-ups in the parking lot of a church.

"I had two sweat suits on plus a hood. We all had hoods. I wasn't trying to hide the fact I was a girl. If it had been a hot day, I would have immediately peeled down to my running suit. But it was a snowy day and so I kept my hood on. We all did. In fact, one of my favorite stories is that when we were walking to the starting line, here comes Will Cloney and he's pushing all the runners inside of this pen. He's saying: 'All right, you runners —get back in the pen.' Cloney came right by and grabbed me on the shoulder and said: 'Move!' He gave me a shove to get in there with the rest of the runners. I was this close to him.

"Well, as soon as I got in there, they could all see I was a woman. 'Hey,' they started saying, 'look at this—a girl! A girl is in the race. Oh, wow!' Everybody started taking pictures and I'm waving to everybody. Now the gun goes off and we start running.

"We're all laughing and joking—I mean, here's the greatest test of my life and now it's actually happening. About the two-mile mark I planned to take off my grubby gray sweats—damn that Jerry Nason. He wrote that I was wearing the crummiest running clothes he ever saw. Of course they were crummy. He should have known that. You don't take good clothes with you if you're going to throw them away.

"I'm ready to take them off because I've got this glorious little maroon outfit on underneath it. All of a sudden the photo truck goes by—it's kind of a flatbed truck, with tiers, and right away they started shooting pictures of me. When they saw I was a girl, they went absolutely crazy. A girl in the race! So now we're all laughing and mugging it up for the cameras when I hear the press bus come up behind us. It goes kind of *shhhhhhhhh* as it comes to a stop. Will Cloney steps down and starts jogging along with us. He gets into an argument with Arnie. He wants to know, 'What's this girl doing in this race?' Arnie says, 'Don't worry about it, I got her in. She's all right.' So I try not to worry about

107

anything. I keep running along, when all of a sudden I hear these footsteps behind me. Sort of scuffling steps. I turn around just as he's about to grab me on the shoulder and spin me around. In the same motion he's trying to grab the number off my suit. 'Get . . . out . . . of . . . my . . . race! You're not supposed to be in my race!' He's just furious. I see this awful face, this awful, angry face, and I'm frightened. I'm really scared. Only once in my life did I ever see my father get angry. I was terrified. Now this man who was grabbing at me, trying to rip the number off my suit—he was the angriest man I've ever seen in my life. I burst into tears. Immediately I started blubbering . . . 'Oh, please, please leave me alone.' With that Arnie starts slapping him with his arms. 'Leave her alone, Jock. Leave her alone,' he said. 'She's my girl. She's okay.' I could see right away that Arnie was helpless. He was as helpless as a sparrow. What I didn't find out until later is that Jock Semple and Arnie ran together. They ran in the Boston Marathon one year and finished something like seventh and eighth, or ninth and tenth, or something like that. Arnie would go over to Jock's house and stay there after the race, have dinner with his family. They'd spend the whole weekend together. They were the best of friends.

"But now here they're both blowing their corks. Jock is screaming at me, 'I'm going to get you out of this race . . . I'm going to get you out!' When all of a sudden here comes Tom—I mean, without a sound, he comes over and hits Jock a cross-body block . . . and it was amazing. Jock went four feet into the air. Honest to goodness, he went right off the ground—literally sailing through the air—and he lands over by the curb in the grass someplace. Now I'm really afraid. We'd knocked him down and I didn't know what to think. He'd assaulted me, but I wasn't thinking of that. I was thinking of him on the ground. Tom was really fuming. Arnie says: 'Run!' We take off like rabbits—*Yeeeeeeeeow!* It's hysterical. We've got twenty-four miles to go and now we're running as fast as we can, as if we could outrace the press bus. Everybody's yapping about it. The Japanese. The Chinese. Yip, yip, yip, yip.

"The press bus stays with us for mile after mile. Now the writers are playing games with us—making up little poems. And what does the "K" stand for—does it stand for Kurt or Karl or Kathy? There was Jock standing on the platform, glaring at us, shaking his fist at us. He kept saying, 'You're . . . in . . . for . . . big

. . . trouble.' That put fear into me. Arnie is yelling, 'Get out of here, Jock. You're not doing us any good now.' I don't think they spoke again for ten whole years.

"The rest of the race was an agony to me. I felt drained. Emotionally drained. Everytime we got to a corner and there'd be a cop standing there, I expected him to step out and arrest us. I thought sure we were headed for jail. Tom really hit him hard. Very hard.

"We lost Tom somewhere along the route—he tried to speed it up and, later, we passed him. When we finally got to the finish line, all the reporters were there and you could see how angry they were, how mad they were that they had to stand out in this rain and wait for us. They were cold and tired. And I wasn't all that cooperative, either. One writer kept asking me if the reason I ran was to help the cause of women. I was so confused. I just wanted to run. I didn't want to prove anything and here all these questions were flying at me. I didn't pay a whole lot of attention to them because I thought they were going to put in a little two-inch article.

"We started back to Syracuse that night and I'll never forget it. It's about two o'clock in the morning and we're on the Thruway when we stop off to get some coffee and hamburgers and ice cream. We're sitting at a counter, like ducks in a row, and we're laughing it up—we ran in the Boston Marathon, ha, ha, ha—when right across the counter from us—it was one of those U-shaped counters —this guy was reading a newspaper. I think it was *The American*. A tabloid. I look over there and suddenly I realize all those pictures on the front page and the back—they were pictures of us. 'Oh oh, that's us, that's us!' I got up and ran around the counter and said to the man, 'Can I see your paper, can I see your paper?' And now we're huddled around looking at all the pictures and trying to read the stories and this guy is sitting there thinking we're some kind of nuts.

"Well, the phone rang off the hook when we got home. It never stopped ringing for a whole week. And I started doing a lot of thinking about it. It was the first time in my life that somebody came down on me that hard just because I was a woman. I wanted to scream at him and say 'Jock, I've been training at least ten miles a day in Syracuse, with snow up to my knees and my eyebrows frozen over, and puking out my guts. I'm an intelligent woman, I'm studying at the university, and I'm here because I love to run.

I love it with a passion. And you're not counting any of those things. You're throwing me out just because I'm a woman.'

"The A.A.U. did the same thing. They said it was against the rules for me to run. I said, 'Why?' They said because it could be harmful. I said, 'How could it be harmful?—I did it and I feel fine. I even beat a couple of men.' They said I had no medical evidence that it wasn't harmful. I told them, 'Then let's get some medical evidence.' They said it wasn't socially acceptable. I told them, 'I'm not in a wrestling match.' I wasn't turning into a firebrand feminist, but I was determined to see that there were some changes made in this system.

"So I ran in every man's race I could find for the next few years and it really got ridiculous. They'd give me a number—'unofficial number 43,' I'd come in first among the women and they'd announce, 'The unofficial women's winner, in unofficial sixty-seventh place in the race, in the unofficial time of . . .' I mean it really got ridiculous.

"Finally, we got it changed. It was just too embarrassing for everyone. Jock finally told us in 1972 that women were now welcome in Boston—we would have dressing rooms, our own doctors, the whole works. He was cold and rather abrupt about it all.

"But the next year—1973—he came right up to me at the starting line and put his arms around me and said: 'Come on, lass. Let's get a wee bit a note-a-rye-a-tee.' "

'Twas the Night Before Boston
by John Linscott

'Twas the night before Boston, and all through the Pru,
The rumors were thick in the land of beef stew.
At noon on the morrow one would break the hex,
A runner would run—of the opposite sex.

A girl in the race? the thought troubled Jock's slumber,
To add insult to injury—she would wear a number.
Jock has sworn by his name—just as firm as a rock,
"Nobody runs—less they're wearing a jock."

Jock scanned all the entries, and medical checks,
Which attested to fitness, but not as to sex.
"Now what's in a name? I'll find one that fits her,"
He checked every name, but he missed one—K. Switzer.

"Ladies, Start Your Engines!"

A "K" could be Karl, or a Kurt, or a Kim.
This "K" stood for Katherine, who's a her, not a him.
So the plot has been hatched, now 'till noon we must wait,
For the big confrontation—our sports Watergate.

On the 19th of April at Hopkinton High,
The runners were dressing with one watchful eye.
They'd heard 'bout the girl, and read all the reports,
One had to be careful when changing his shorts.

But as the time passed, and the noon hour was nigh,
No runner appeared with a mascara'd eye.
Nor with legs that weren't hairy, were slender, not bowed,
Yes, a female was rumored—but nobody showed.

Well, the gun it was fired, after all of the fuss,
Jock sighed with relief, and mounted the bus.
"Thank God there's no woman to mess up my race,
"Imagine a runner in shorts—hemmed with lace."

But there in the pack with a shape and a curl,
Jock spied Miss K. Switzer and he cried, "It's a girl!
"They're all right to dance with the Charleston or rhumba,
But girls can't run Boston while wearing a number."

So he sprang from the bus to collar the phony,
As he leaped to the pavement from the grasp of Will Cloney.
He weaved through the pack like a hound on the hunt,
Now he grasps for her number—no Jock—not from the front!

Now advancing toward Jock and before he could pull back,
Came a friend of fair Kathy, who was built like a fullback.
They met there at noon on the Marathon course,
The gritty old Scot—the immovable force.

The damsel was saved, and she sped on her way,
The story's been told and retold to this day.
And I heard Jock exclaim as she ran out of sight,
"I think I was hit—by a woman's right."

13
Our Not So Jolly
Jock

"I don't discriminate against women. They're just not allowed to run
in my race."

—John D. Semple
N.S.D.P. (Not So Distant Past)

FIRST OF ALL, there are two things you should know about Jock
Semple. He doesn't own the Boston Marathon (though it seems that
way) and his bark is worse than his bite (which seems that way,
too).

So don't be too hard on Jock. He loves this race, and now, he
loves the ladies, too. So he's got a temper. Two out of three ain't bad.

Jock Semple has been called a lot of things, by a lot of people,
over the years. Some of them even to his face. Irascible? Yes. Irri-
table? Yes. Annoying? You've got the point.

But he cares. He cares about marathon running and he cares
about this race and these days it's hard to find people who care
about anything.

Jock has been called the "Man in the Middle." He has been
called the "Angry Overseer of the Marathon." Both titles are correct.

When you want to call Boston and talk to somebody about the
Boston Marathon, the operator puts you through to Jock Semple.
Don't ask me how it works. But it does.

More often than not, you'll catch him in the middle of giving a
rubdown at his one-man massage parlor in the Boston Garden. Or

112

worse, you'll get him just after the morning mail comes in and he's sitting there looking at a pile of letters—entries from all over the United States—and trying to figure out which ones are the phonies, and getting madder by the minute because he knows some of them are trying to put one over on him and he can't figure out which ones are the culprits. A lot of people try to crash the Marathon, which is sort of silly, because they can just get out there and run, with or without Jock Semple's consent. But they don't get numbers and they don't get their names in the newspapers and for some—you'd be surprised at how many— that's all the Boston Marathon means to them. A moment of fame, however fleeting.

Jock is at his best on the phone, though.

"Oh, so you wanna run in the Marathon, do you? One thing you just might do is try runnin' twenty-six miles t' see if you can . . . Oh, y'know y'can, do ya? Well, then, tell me, what kind of time you plannin' to do the Marathon in . . .? Two-ten!"

(The record is 2:09.55, held by Billy Rodgers, and now Jock's face is turning crimson.)

"Well, forget the whole thing, 'cause yer not worthy o' the event, and we doon't want t' hear any more o' yer crap."

Bam!

That's the receiver going back on the hook.

Brrrrrrr.

That's the poor guy on the rubbing table, hoping that Jock can get a handle on himself before he gets to working on his back again.

Jock Semple will be remembered forevermore as the angry man—"Oh, that angry face!"—who tried to push Kathy Switzer off the course in 1967. He says all he was doing was trying to rip the numbers off her sweat suit because at that time women were not welcome in the Boston Marathon. The pictures were printed everywhere from Boston to Bangkok and Jock became the villain of his time.

Myron Cope, a writer from Pittsburgh, would capture Jock Semple better than anyone in creation. The year after the shoving incident Cope visited Semple in his office—not more than a couple of musty rooms down a darkened corridor in the Boston Garden —and asked Jock about pushing the girl.

"I'm not o'poozed t' women's athletics," Jock was to tell him, with a Scottish burr as thick as the day he left Clydebank for America back in 1923. "But we're taught t' respect laws—t' respect rules. The amateur rules here say a woman can't run more th'n a mile and a half. I'm in favor of makin' their races longer, but they doon't belong with men. They doon't belong runnin' with Jim Ryun. You wouldn't like t' see a woman runnin' with Jim Ryun, wouldya?"

Jock Semple, like Will Cloney and all the others who are involved in the staging of this race, works for nothing. It is truly a labor of love. Jock will tell you that Cloney gets it only one day a year, while he has to put up with the letters and phone calls 365 days a year. He doesn't say exactly who calls him on Christmas Day.

Most of the runners know Jock as the guy who stands outside the buses going to Hopkinton the morning of the race. He's the one with the shopping bag in his hand, saying, "In here . . . In here!" as he collects their two bucks for the ride.

Jock is past seventy now, and while he threatens to quit every year—"these phones are drivin' me batty, let me tell ye"—he always comes back for one more race. He has been involved with the Boston Marathon since 1929, as a runner, then as a coach, and now as a one-man-answering-service-and-screening-committee.

His finest moment came in 1930. He finished seventh. He hitch-hiked from Philadelphia to Boston and ran right with the leaders most of the way. He knew there were gold medals awaiting the first eight finishers. When he got up to eighth place, he turned it on and came home seventh. His mother was waiting for him at the finish line [and could there be many greater success stories than that written in this country?]

"Well, I got a bit of a' lump in me throat," says Jock.

That lump has never gone away. Jock jumps in with both feet, even if he says nothing more on the phone than, "Send in a self-addressed stamped envelope—I'll tell yer only one more time: a self-addressed stamped envelope!"

Bam!

On the day of the race, Will Cloney gives a little speech on the bus ride out to Hopkinton. It's not exactly Rockne talking to the Fighting Irish but it goes something like this:

"Now, Jock, take it easy today. Don't get nervous. Everything's

The people's choice, 69-year-old Johnny Kelley, hears the applause of his fans as he nears the finish line. (Photo by John Castagno)

The "Great Shoving Incident" in the 1967 race takes place as (*left*) Jock Semple closes in on Kathy Switzer in an attempt to tear the number from her running suit. Tom Miller (*center photo*) slams into Jock and (*right*) sends the old Scot flying off to the side of the road. (United Press International)

And here's Kathy Switzer sprinting across the finish line—wheeeeeee! I'm a woman and I'm alive and I'm allowed to run. (*Runner's World*)

Now accepted as an official entry in 1972, Kathy Switzer—ever the female—takes a moment to adjust her hair-do. Never know when you'll have to look good for the cameras. (Associated Press)

Nina Kuscsik is about to become the first official woman's winner in 1972. (*Boston Globe* Photo)

Kim Merritt nearing her date with destiny—the woman's champion of 1976. (*Boston Globe* Photo)

Here's Will Rodgers on the way to his 1975 record-shattering victory.
(*Boston Globe* Photo)

Rodgers stops for a drink of water. Aren't you supposed to drink on the run? "The cup spills if I run," says Rodgers. (*Boston Globe* Photo)

Now Rodgers stops to tie his shoelace, kneeling on his gloves. He stopped *five times* during his run—four for water, once for his right shoe. (*Boston Globe* Photo)

Jock Semple gives the word to Rodgers: "Git goin', lad! Yee'v got a chance for the'r record!" (*Boston Globe* Photo)

(RIGHT) Rodgers gets the best reward of all from his wife-to-be, Ellen. The somber marathon writer looking on is your author. (*Boston Globe* Photo)

(BELOW) No, that's not the President of the United States. That's Will Rodgers sprinting for the finish line in front of the Big Pru for a record-breaking time of 2 hours 9 minutes 55 seconds. (*Boston Globe* Photo)

going to be all right. Do you hear me now—don't get excited. Everything's going to work out all right."

Jock sits there and nods. Then he sees those long lines for the seven toilets in the Hopkinton gym and the red starts to rise in his face.

Actually, Jock Semple is an accomplished masseur—a physiotherapist, if you please. He probably has the most unusual clientele in all Boston, if not the whole East Coast. Both bankers and boxers see him, and Jock rubs them all. The morning Myron Cope was in to visit him, Jock took his lunch—a meatloaf sandwich and a Thermos of coffee—and stuffed it behind the radiator to keep it warm.

Clif Keane, the caustic Boston writer, once said of Jock Semple's Massage Parlor: "Jock throws them into a big pot of steam and cooks them. I don't think he goes in too heavy for those newfangled machines. Every once in a while, when I wasn't feeling well, I'd go in and let him give me a punch in the back, but the day he grilled a cheese sandwich on the radiator, that was enough for me."

Down the hall from this outpost of purity are the offices of the Boston Celtics, where Red Auerbach sits and thinks. And wonders how the hell Jock and those guys do it.

"What's their race prove?" says Auerbach. "So you prove you can run a long time, so what? If you're running to keep in shape, run two miles maybe. Okay. But this! Twenty-six miles! You gotta be a nut."

Auerbach is no stranger to the Boston Marathon. He used to live at the Lenox Hotel, where the race would finish, and he'd stand by the window and watch these guys come running over the finish line and all but collapse into somebody's arms.

"I used to stand there saying, 'What the hell is this?' All those bastards were running for nothing. They ran twenty-six miles for a cup of beef stew, a cupcake and a glass of milk. It didn't make sense.

"I followed them into the hotel once. I was curious to have a look, figuring they'd have a special chef behind the counter with a great pile of steaming stew. They were pouring it out of *cans*! It was goddamned *canned* beef stew! I couldn't believe it."

But then, could Red Auerbach ever hope to understand Jock Semple, who didn't even stop for stew.

God bless Jock, and don't be too harsh on him. So he shoved a girl once. He apologized. Well, sort of. He gave her a big smooch for the cameras a few years later. Jock's been shoving people off the course for years. Bicycles. Motorcycles. Wagons.

One year he shoved a cop. That's when Will Cloney started giving his speech again.

14
Will Cloney:
Man Behind the Scenes

IF THE NATIONAL FOOTBALL LEAGUE can have a czar in Pete Rozelle and baseball a czar in Bowie Kuhn, it seems only fair that the world's most celebrated footrace should have a czar.

Only don't call Will Cloney that to his face. Not that he'll get mad. It takes a whole lot to make him mad. He is a kind man, a genteel man, a thoughtful man, a generous man. But if anyone holds this whole race together, it is this ex-sportswriter who happens to love sports, especially runners, and most of all, this race.

Could you imagine, say, an Alan Eagelson, the prominent player-agent, serving as "director" of the Boston Marathon? He'd sit there, stupefied. Nobody gets paid. Nobody makes any money. Nobody negotiates contracts. Nobody works out TV packages. In the Boston Marathon, nobody runs out their option.

This is the one simon-pure athletic event left in the United States. The Boston Marathon draws more people than the Kentucky Derby or the Indianapolis 500 and it doesn't cost anyone a cent to see it. This is the charm of the old race. That it is so devoid of commercialism. The closest anyone comes to getting a plug is the Prudential Insurance Company, which has done a mighty job in recent years handling all of those exhausted runners at the finish line. Prudential is mentioned in this book but only through the thrust of the author. Nobody at Pru tried to cash in on any publicity. It comes to them honestly.

And so it is with Will Cloney, without whose help it would have been difficult to get this account down on paper. Will planned to write a Marathon book himself and could have easily been upset by having an outsider come in and record the history of this race. But like everyone else who was encountered in Boston —from Frank Moloney at the Public Library to George Collins in the library of the *Boston Globe*—the author received only the utmost cooperation. He also got a smile from these people and that was important, too.

The Boston Marathon is a labor of love for Cloney. He wrote sports in Boston until his paper, the *Post,* went out of business. This was in 1946 and, seeing little future in the writing business, Cloney turned to high finance and caught on with Keystone Custodian Funds, Inc., where he rose to be vice president. Once each year—with his boss's approval—Cloney turns his attention to the Boston Marathon. He was close to the Brown family, the founders of the race, and feels somebody has to keep the race alive and well.

The first thing Cloney tells you is that he doesn't do it alone. None of that czar stuff. He holds the title of "director," but he has had considerable help through the years, notably from other dedicated men like Jock Semple. If Cloney is the director of the B.A.A. race, Jock is its "conscience." "We canna handle too many more runners," the exasperated Jock will say, and then go ahead and handle them.

Cloney has been on the job for three decades and hasn't made a penny out of it. The runners know him and that is enough of a reward. To see that moon-like face one more time—maybe smiling, maybe frowning—is a comfort to every runner who has been to Boston more than one time.

"I just think that somewhere along the line you have to give something back," says Cloney. "The race brings out a tremendous amount of positive publicity for Boston, which might help make up for some of the unpleasant notices that the city has received in recent years. I just do what I can."

Cloney graduated from Harvard in 1933. He went into sports writing and also taught journalism at Northeastern University. He will talk marathoning with you long past his lunch hour. The boss understands that, too. Cloney has been around the race for more than fifty years. He covered it along with Jerry Nason and grew to know the two Johnny Kelleys, Les Pawson, Tarzan Brown, Gerard Cote, Joe Smith and all of the other legendary figures who have made the Boston Marathon what it is. And like a true official of the race he worries that this great classic may collapse from the sheer number of competitors. It is one thing to handle two hundred runners but quite another to handle two thousand. That's why the Prudential and Honeywell corporations have been so important in recent years. No longer can you stand at the finish line and check them off by pencil. *Whirrrrrr. Zzzzzzzzzz. Click. Click.* You feed the data into the computers and out come the results.

Here's what Will Cloney says about the race:

"I think you can call the Boston Marathon the last stronghold of unadulterated amateurism in the country. We attract some of the world's great distance runners, but we get thousands whose only desire is to compete and—they hope—finish. The Marathon is an anachronism in this age of automation. At a time when most people won't walk if they can ride, we've got thousands of men—and now women, too—who train for months just to test themselves in this race.

"By professional standards, I guess you'd have to say our prizes are rather modest—but in their own way they are priceless. The winner gets a laurel wreath, usually bestowed on him by the mayor of Boston or the governor of the Commonwealth of Massachusetts. He also receives a diamond-studded solid-gold sunburst medal. This is a specially designed award that hangs from a gold and blue ribbon, which are the colors of the B.A.A. To a runner, it's like the Medal of Honor, the Croix de Guerre.

"We try to recognize as many runners as we can. The next nine finishers get trophies, as well as the first three women finishers. The next 75 get medals and we've even got a team trophy.

"Actually, the international magnetism of the race is amazing because we pay none of the expenses for anyone. You'll find ethnic groups all over the country getting together to send one of their runners to Boston. For instance, the fine Finnish groups in Massachusetts, Rhode Island and Connecticut will raise money to bring one or two of the top Finns to the Boston race.

"Japan has been sending athletes over for years now and many of the Japanese-Americans living in the Boston area help out with accommodations for these runners. Back in 1947, when America was deep in the fighting in Korea, our G.I.'s over there contributed to a purse to send Yun Bok Suh to Boston, and the youngster promptly won the race.

"Logistically, the race is a nightmare. It requires the generosity of the town of Hopkinton in providing dressing quarters at the start, the cooperation of a dozen police departments along the way —as well as of the State Police—and I don't know how we'd make it without the help of the Prudential people.

"The competitors fall into three categories: the ones who train faithfully, running thousands of practice miles and qualifying as topflight athletes in their own specialty; the ones who have legitimate hopes but lack the physical resources, and the ones who enter for the sheer fun of it, on a bet perhaps, or to get their name in the paper, or simply to be a part—if only for a few miles —of the greatest race of its kind. Actually, we're no crazier than the businessmen who play thirty-six holes of golf or the fellow who kills himself going through four or five sets of tennis on a scorching afternoon.

"The lure of the Marathon is something else. Maybe this is why the late Pat Dengis, a highly skilled aircraft technician, took time off from his job in Baltimore to shoot for the B.A.A. crown. Pat won every other race in America, but the best he could do in Boston was second. His death in a crash on a test flight in 1948 put an end to his lifelong ambition to win just once in Boston.

"And maybe this is why a highly intelligent person like Lou Gregory, a principal at Manlius High School in New York, came here even after he was in the Navy, as a lieutenant, and kept coming back year after year, hoping he could win just once.

"The runners never know what's going to greet them in Boston. April in Boston is not the most predictable time of the year. They've had to run in snow and sleet and hail and wind and rain. Sometimes it's an inferno out there. Sometimes it is a gorgeous spring day and you forget all the others.

"The medical profession has always been interested in our race.

They wonder why we attract so many runners and what happens to them during the race. In 1928 a group of three doctors—one of them from Belgium—conducted a series of tests at the finish line to see if the race caused 'athlete's heart.' They found out that in no case did the heart become larger, as some thought, but in fact became smaller in some instances.

"We've had to put in rules to keep the field down and the hardest part is telling a marathon runner he can't run. Sometimes I wonder how we get through it all. Sometimes I think this is my last year. But the moment the race is over, I start thinking about next year. It is a really beautiful thing, this race."

15

Ted Corbitt:
Man of Iron

TED CORBITT REMEMBERS as a kid running to and from school—
and not just because he liked to run. Black kids weren't even
allowed on buses then. At least not in Dunbarton, South Carolina,
in the flat, hot Savannah River basin country. But that isn't why
Young Ted ran all the way. There were hazards along the way—
rattlers, copperheads, water moccasins and corals—and he could
do without being bitten by any of these poisonous snakes. It seems
like Ted Corbitt has been running for his entire life. He may be
the mightiest marathoner of them all.

"Oh, you're not going to write about me, are you?" he said at
his home in the Bronx in New York City. "I didn't do very much."

In the matter of winning Boston Marathons, he didn't do anything. He ran in twenty-two of them and never came in on top.
Sixth was the best he could ever do. But you don't measure this
man in the matter of winning races. Victories, yes. Ted Corbitt
has been scoring one victory after another for his entire life. He
has conquered himself almost every day he has lived. He has
proven that the black man can run great distances, a feat few
thought they could do.

Statistic: Ted Corbitt has run in 181 marathons. He has completed 181 marathons. Not Clarence H. DeMar, not Johnny (The Elder) Kelley, not Tarzan Brown—not any of the great distance runners of our country can make that statement. To finish every marathon he ever started is an almost unbelievable feat. In his way, Ted Corbitt is an almost unbelievable man.

As a rule, black athletes (except for the Africans) do not make great distance runners. Why, nobody is quite sure. They are without equal in the dashes—dazzling record setters. But you don't find many of them trudging along the back roads of New England headed for the distant finish line in downtown Boston. Why blacks don't run distances—or don't care to—nobody knows. You can get all sorts of theories, one stranger than the next. A runner told me, "I think it's because they've been suppressed for so long—they want it all *now*. They want to catch up in a hurry. They don't have time to slog along any more." Fiction or fact? Who can say. But the blacks just don't run the distances the same as the whites or the Orientals or even the Indians. Corbitt, who is now fifty-six years old, is an exception.

Statistic: Ted Corbitt ran in his first Boston Marathon at the age of thirty-one.

Statistic: Ted Corbitt ran in a one hundred-mile race . . . and finished third . . . at the age of forty-nine.

Statistic: Ted Corbitt ran in a twenty-hour race . . . and again finished third . . . at the age of fifty-three.

Statistic: Ted Corbitt ran in his most recent Boston Marathon (1974) at the age of fifty-four.

He may indeed be the mightiest marathoner of them all.

Corbitt, a quiet, almost introverted man, merely smiles about his accomplishments—especially his durability.

"I didn't run very well in some of those races, not what I wanted to do. And I suppose one day, I'll just pull up before I'm finished and walk off the course and that'll be the end of it."

But don't bet on it, for this is a man of fierce pride and great determination. Can you imagine running for twenty-four hours at the age of fifty-three? Corbitt did it in Great Britain on November 3-4, 1973—a distance of 134.7 miles.

He says he'll be back in the Boston Marathon as soon as he is over his assorted ills and ailments. He didn't run much in 1976, but if he says he'll be back, he'll be back.

"Fitness can't be stored," said Corbitt. "It must be earned over and over, indefinitely. If a man runs for twenty years and stops completely, it is just a matter of time until he is in the same physical condition as the fellow who has never done anything."

Corbitt represented the United States in the 1952 Olympics in Helsinki. He finished forty-fourth in the marathon. He failed to ever again make the team, but it wasn't because he didn't try.

Imagine the punishment he inflicted upon himself when he tried to win a place on the 1956 U.S. team. He laid out a demanding four-year plan for himself. In 1952 he ran a total of 2,850 miles. The next year he ran 2,398 miles. Then, in 1954, he ran every day for the entire year: 540 workouts for 5,145 miles. In 1955 he made his big push and worked out no fewer than 790 times for 5,182 miles. He was named the first alternate on a three-man team and watched from the sidelines when the big race was run.

You will never hear any remorse in this man's voice. He has punished himself, but he also has enjoyed his years as a runner.

"I've been very lucky for my entire life," he said. Ted Corbitt was doing his thing long before many blacks were accorded even the most basic freedoms.

As a youngster, Corbitt was taught by his parents that if he was going to do anything in life, it was worth doing well—to the best of his ability. Even when his family moved out of South Carolina to a tough slum section of Cincinnati, where alcoholism, unemployment and racism were rampant, young Ted already began forming the character that would carry him great distances in life. He ran his first race at the age of thirteen in an intramural track meet at school. It was a sixty-yard dash and the other youngsters must have been amused by this new boy in their presence. Young Ted showed up dressed in corduroy pants, long underwear and no shoes. He won the race.

Through most of his early years Corbitt was a sprint man, like most young blacks. Soon he was running to and from school— about a fifty-minute trip—just to save carfare.

In 1941 Corbitt underwent a physical for military service and to his utter disbelief he was found to be suffering from tuberculosis. As a senior in high school he had experienced long seizures of euphoria but thought nothing of it. He thought it was a by-product of all his running. X rays showed that his right lung was badly scarred. So, instead of entering the service, he went to work in a cookie factory, taking the night shift so he could do some running during the day. Ted was re-examined in 1944 and this time he was found physically fit. He entered the service and just as his ship reached Okinawa, word was received of the atomic bombings of Hiroshima and Nagasaki. He longed to run through the beautiful hilly terrain of Okinawa, but there was still enemy resistance on the island and so he remained close to camp.

When he returned home—he was then living in New York—Ted still had a great desire to run, but he was torn between this desire and the necessity of earning a living. He attended New York University, earning a master's degree in physical education, and more or less jogged in his spare time. When he finished school, in 1950, he found his evenings were free and it was then that he pursued running with his entire being.

Ted Corbitt had always had a dream—a dream of excelling at something, just as his parents had advised. He found his thoughts turning to the Boston Marathon. He was intrigued by the stories of the great Narragansett Indian Tarzan Brown—how he ran through the rain to win this great race. He wondered how anyone could run that far. He wondered if he could do it himself. In the meantime, he kept his dream alive by keeping a scrapbook of the Boston Marathon.

At this point in his life not much was known about long-distance runners. Ted knew of no other runners who could give him advice. So he began reading every book on the subject that he could lay his hands on. The philosophies of one man stood out among them all: Emil Zatopek of Czechoslovakia. One day Corbitt would stand at the starting line of the Olympic marathon and hear Zatopek say to the other runners, "Men, today we die a little." Now, as he was into serious training as a distance runner, Ted was incorporating two of Zatopek's principal philosophies—progression and resistance. According to the great Czech runner, the body could adjust to any workload if the runner moves up to it in progressive steps. It was easier read than done for Ted Corbitt.

He ran with heavy boots and suffered bruised legs and painful blisters. His lungs ached for air. Slowly, he began to conquer himself—to gain the mastery that was required to run long distances.

Still, he was a novice. He did not understand the processes of dehydration. He couldn't figure out why his body would begin rebelling at around the fifteen-mile mark. One day, while running in the snow, he was breathing heavily and unconsciously stuck his tongue out to catch the snowflakes. Then it dawned on him. He was thirsty! Until then he never touched liquids during a work-out. He felt they were harmful to him. But from the moment he began to drink water as he ran, his capacity quickly increased—until that memorable day in 1952 when he competed in his first Boston Marathon.

In later years John Chodes—an author-runner—did a beautiful book about Corbitt, much of which is in this chapter. Chodes, a playwright as well as a novelist, recounted Corbitt's first effort in Boston:

With one day remaining, Ted went by train to Boston and stayed at a hotel in Back Bay, near the finish. When he awoke in the morning his heart was pounding.

Corbitt had no illusions about his prospects. His only concern was finishing and in under three hours. He was aware that New York and New England alone were saturated with super-talented runners who would finish far ahead.

The excitement and tension mounted when he reached the starting line in the small, quiet village of Hopkinton. Here, one hundred and fifty marathon men from Japan, Canada, Turkey and all parts of the United States had gathered.

Ted knew few of the starters. He stood alone, waiting for the gun. He was awed by the stature of the race and by the dozen overseas stars who had traveled thousands of miles to compete in this classic.

Then the gun cracked and there was a mad scramble for the lead. For a mile or two Ted was pulled along the lonely two-lane road by the excitement of the scramble. Then he settled down and moved along in fortieth place.

The first test of his resolve wasn't long in coming. After six miles on the winding, rolling road, just as the field passed through the town of Framingham, Ted was struck with a severe stitch. It burned at his side and slowed him down. After a few rugged miles it eased and he increased the pace again. He was now well into the run and the sweat soaked through his shirt. It was cool and cloudy and a refreshing wind gently pushed him along.

Near halfway they passed through the college town of Wellesley and dipped into a long valley of several miles. Here again he was tormented by another stitch, but he bravely ran through this second episode. He slowed again but when the pain subsided he found he was too tired to run as fast as earlier.

Beyond halfway he knew he was in a marathon. He was dehydrating and craved a drink but feared the intake of water might cramp his stomach. As in training, his lack of water exhausted him.

This one section, the valley of the Newton Hills, between twelve and seventeen miles, reminded Ted of Dante's *Inferno*. He was very tired, but here he passed dozens of runners in various stages of extreme exhaustion. Some were bent over or trotted weakly. Others staggered unevenly along the road. Others walked, some sat down on the curb.

Ted was not in all that much better condition, but he was moving steadily as he started the long punishing four-mile stretch through the Newton Hills. Once over the longest grade, 'Heartbreak Hill,' Ted was severely fatigued. Even within the final five miles of sprawling Boston itself, he was not confident and still doubted he would make it. At twenty-three miles he had to consciously move one leg after the other.

With two miles remaining, his right hamstring started cramping, another dehydration symptom. This shortened his stride and forced a slower pace. In the last mile he was folding up at every step. As he turned onto Exeter Street and the finish line, he was on the verge of staggering, but he had made it. He was dazed but happy. He had conquered the distance. He had finished fifteenth.

This was the first of many such conquests for Corbitt in the Boston ·Marathon. He would run almost every year for more than the next two decades—even once when the doctors found him "physically unfit." That was the wildest day of all for him.

He had run strongly, if not brilliantly, for five years, finishing sixth, eleventh, eleventh, sixth and eleventh. But 1958 proved to be a nightmare year for him. He began suffering from acute diarrhea any time he tried to run more than six miles. He fought the ailment, even trying to overcome it by not eating the day before a race. It was only through the aid of Dr. William Ruthrauff —the man who invented Pepsodent toothpaste—that Corbitt was able to overcome his ailment. The doctor had found this ailment in other runners, a result of longtime exertion on the body. He neutralized it by filling Ted with vitamin B, mostly in the form of yogurt and buttermilk. The ailment would plague Corbitt for the remainder of his career, but he was able to keep it under control.

But now, 1958, he doped things out in Boston and saw a chance that he could finish as high as third place. He was so turned on by the prospect that his heart was pounding strongly on the morning of the race. He appeared calm on the outside, but when the doctors put their stethoscopes to his chest, their eyes almost bugged out. His heart was hammering away at 140 beats a minute. They disqualified him.

Ted protested. He argued that he was a qualified marathon runner and how could a qualified marathon runner have a faulty heart. It turned out that Ted was preparing himself for a war but didn't know it. It also turned out that Al Confalone and Johnny Lafferty, two other prominent runners, also were disqualified by the doctors.

A great disagreement arose, with the officials arguing in behalf of the runners and the physicians holding firm in their stand. Ted was headed back to the dressing room to get his clothes when Lafferty and Confalone talked him into running "for the fun of it."

Corbitt went the full distance and was an unofficial sixth-place finisher. Lafferty was seventh and Confalone ninth and the physicians felt embarrassed. They listened to Corbitt's heart again—and again it was still pounding. One of the doctors said, "The longer I listen the faster it gets." After this strange experience, Corbitt always brought a pile of medical certificates with him to prove he was healthy. He would never be rejected again.

Corbitt became a familiar figure in the Boston Marathon, a favorite with the mobs along the way. "Hey, there goes old man Corbitt!" "Hey, Corbitt, ain't you ever going to quit?" He would wave at them and smile and they would smile back.

Retire?

Corbitt told Chodes, his biographer, "No, I'm not going to retire. I've got a few more things left to do. I want to run in the Pike's Peak Marathon, I want to walk one hundred miles in less than twenty-four hours, I want to walk 50 miles on a track, I want to run back-to-back marathons, I want to run another twenty-four hour race, I want to . . ."

16
Marathon Marriages

MARTIN KRAFT IS A water-meter reader. He used to drink, smoke and sleep a lot. Mostly naps in the afternoon. He'd come home from a day on the job—maybe two hundred houses . . . down 10 steps, up ten steps . . . and he'd be tired out.

So he'd have lunch, take a nap, get up and have dinner and then squat before the TV set until it was time to go to bed.

Life was a drag.

He never felt good. No pep. No pizzazz. It was the same thing every day. It seemed the more he slept, the more tired he got.

Then he and his wife, Alexa, began jogging. Nothing big. Around the block once. Maybe twice.

It hurt.

"I'd come in and feel my back had gone out on me or that there was something wrong with my kidneys. I felt terrible," said Martin Kraft.

His wife, meanwhile, had met this "dizzy blonde" at nursery school—a gal named Jeanne Bocci. She was a runner. She spoke of doing her ten miles a day and Alexa would sit there and think Jeanne Bocci was half out of her mind.

Ten miles a day?

Alexa Kraft was satisfied with once around the block. The same with Martin.

Their life was about to change—drastically.

The Boccis—Jeanne and Jerry—were both runners and they invited the Krafts to come over to Belle Isle to watch one of their marathons. Belle Isle is situated in the Detroit River between Detroit and Windsor, Canada.

Alexa and Martin went to take a look and their eyes almost fell out of their heads. Here were all these "goofy looking people in shorts" and they were going around and around the island.

Jeanne Bocci invited Alexa to run with her for a while. Alexa went maybe a mile, then got back into the car with her husband. They preferred to drive, thank you.

"I couldn't believe it," said Martin Kraft. "I watched these guys going around the island, running over the small bridges, and they were going faster after twenty miles than I ever could run for one mile. I thought to myself, 'Man, I can never do that.'"

In 1976 Alexa and Martin Kraft ran in their first Boston Marathon. In all of that oppressive heat, Martin Kraft finished in 2 hours 59 minutes 55 seconds, earning a certificate of accomplishment by five seconds. His wife came in a little more than a half hour later, at 3:34, but she was just as pleased as her husband. She had finished the race, gone the entire route, despite the blazing sun and the temperature that hovered in the middle nineties.

All of this after only a year and a half of running.

"I feel so much better now it's unbelievable," said Martin Kraft. "My weight got up to one hundred and sixty-five and I never weighed that much in my life. I was tired all the time. I was lethargic. I began to think that maybe I should get out and run a little more. I figured maybe that's why people are tired all the time. They lay around too much.

"When your sugar starts to drop off, you sit down and have a cup of coffee and a donut or a sweet roll. It gives you a momentary lift but pretty soon you're tired again.

"What do they do with kids in school? They don't stop for a coffee break. They have a recess. They get them up and moving around.

"I figured maybe that's what I should do—and now I've never felt better in my life. Now I read my water meters better than ever," Martin Kraft smiled.

It is hard to imagine how anyone can go from no running at all to completing a Boston Marathon within 18 months time. The Krafts are proof that running can aid a marriage and lead to a happier life.

Before Martin Kraft took up running he'd find himself not wanting to get out of bed in the morning.

"I'd phone in sick . . . I missed thirteen days in 14 months and my boss finally sent me a letter pointing this out to me," he said. "Since taking up running, I've had only two sick days in the last fifteen months . . ." That's because he was sore after running in his first Boston Marathon.

It was well worth the effort, for now Martin Kraft is filled with life—busier than ever around his home, in his job and in the neighborhood.

He said: "I don't think running is socially acceptable, not yet anyway. People still look down on us as sort of creepy. For instance, Alexa's sister thinks we're nuts."

"That's right," said Alexa. "We run seven days a week—I do it in the morning and Martin does it in the afternoon or the evening. My sister says she couldn't get up five mornings a week, much less seven. And to run ten miles a day—she thinks we're both out of our minds."

Maybe so. But the Krafts' have three small children—ages six, four and two—and the kids were swirling all around them during the interview and Alexa and Martin never once lost their patience with them.

"It's strange to say, but we're better people now," said Martin. "I know we're a lot closer."

For one thing, their sex life has improved.

"That's true," smiled Alexa. "When I first started running, I'd get so tired that I couldn't wait until I got to bed. Martin knew this, so he'd make me sit on the bottom step of the stairs until he was ready to go to bed. Then we'd go upstairs together.

"Now," she added, "we both feel good *all* the time."

The Krafts have been married nine years. Both are twenty-nine. It's uncommon for both husband and wife to run, but they see it as the beginning of a trend.

"It's like my sister says," smiles Alexa, "it's a good thing we're both involved—not just one of us."

The Krafts drove to their first Boston Marathon with the Boccis

—another husband and wife team. The strategy was for the husbands to take off and run together and the wives to lay back and run at their own pace.

Incredibly enough, out of the more than two thousand runners in the race, Alexa Kraft and Jeanne Bocci wound up with their pictures spread across the top of the sports section of the *Boston Globe*.

It was a two thousand to one chance . . . or two thousand to two —but there they were in their homemade head coverings, looking like a couple of Egyptian dancers appearing at the Club Nile.

That was the big problem—what to wear on their heads? They knew it would be hot and everyone cautioned them to cover their heads. But the group did not arrive in Boston until Saturday night and all the stores were closed. They were not open on Sunday and there would be no time on Monday—the day of the race—to go out and buy head coverings.

So the gals—as with all women in history—spent most of their time designing their own hat styles. These were cut out of T-shirts and fit snugly, but with an opening in the back so they could stuff ice cubes under the covering.

It must have worked, because while 40 percent of the field did not finish the race (as compared with 13 percent the previous year), Alexa Kraft and Jeanne Bocci made it all the way.

The only one who had any real trouble was Jerry Bocci and he was the most experienced runner of all. He has been at it since the age of thirteen. He's now thirty-nine.

It was just too hot for Jerry Bocci and so he waited up for the girls and the three of them crossed the finish line holding hands, a nice touch for the newcomer, Alexa.

Martin Kraft, who finished under the three-hour deadline, couldn't understand the plight of the others. He got four bowls of beef stew and when the gals couldn't even look at theirs, he ate their stew as well as his own.

Actually, these two couples have been drawn together by the common bond of running.

The Boccis stage their own race every New Year's Eve. It's held down at Windmill Point in Grosse Point, a posh suburb to the east of Detroit. It's a four-mile trek—a mile out and a mile back. Everyone does it twice. Then they all go over to the Boccis' for the awards and a spaghetti dinner to welcome in the New Year.

"I think the Boccis' party is what really sold me on running," said Martin Kraft. "They must have had one hundred fifty in their house. It wasn't a very big house and they were everywhere—in the living room, in the rec room downstairs—even up in the children's bedroom. It was a racially mixed group, but there were no animosities there at all. Even the few wives who did some smoking didn't smoke as much as they probably wanted to. Running can do this to people, even indirectly."

Jerry Bocci was asked a rather difficult question: How can a guy who is forty-eight years old and thirty-five pounds overweight and has been out of shape his entire adult life . . . how can someone like this begin running? He was not asked for a clinical approach—just how he would go about showing somebody to run after spending twenty-five years of his own life at the sport.

He gave the author the following ten-step program:

1. Meet me at the track at five o'clock tomorrow afternoon and bring a sweat suit and sneakers.

2. We'll start out by jogging twenty yards and walking twenty yards. Oh, you can't jog twenty yards? Let's start with ten or even five. Jog five yards, then walk five yards . . . until you've made the tour of the track. Stay on the grass, if possible, because it's going to hurt enough anyway.

3. When you can get it up to twenty yards, do it. But don't push yourself. Always match the running distance with the same walking distance.

4. Expect to be sore. But don't be dismayed by it. The worst part is at the beginning. Everything may hurt.

5. Get out every day, no matter what. That's the most important factor—not how far you run or how fast, just be sure to do it every day.

6. When it starts getting a little easier—say, when you can jog thirty yards and walk thirty yards—aim to get it to the point where you can jog around the track at least once. But again, don't rush yourself. Just make sure you do a little every day.

7. Cut down on the meals. Eat, but not so much.

8. When you've got it up to one tour of the track, add on a little each day. When you finally make it to a mile, look for other places to run so that you aren't bored by your surroundings.

9. Now don't be surprised if you can't get past one or two miles. A lot of people never make it beyond that barrier. It is too bad,

because one to two miles can be a drag. Usually there's very little joy in it. The fun comes—and this is what most non-runners don't understand—if you can ever get beyond two miles. You just seem to relax and the next two or three miles can be genuine fun. In other words, it's easier—and more enjoyable—to be able to run five or six miles than it is one or two.

10. Finally, just go out every day and enjoy the sights and sounds of your world. It's a pretty nice place. You ought to take a look at it.

17

Scouting Report:
Bad Eyes, Good Legs,
Strong Heart

JOE PARDO IS BLIND, so it was a little frustrating running his first Boston Marathon.

Not because he couldn't see where he was going, but because nobody could keep up with him.

Joe, who works as a masseur at the Y.M.C.A. in Flushing, New York, always had this dream and his dream always wore sneakers. He didn't want to be the President or a doctor or a lawyer. Joe wanted to be a jock.

He couldn't play second base because how do you pivot on the DP and get the ball over to first base? So he decided to run. You don't need eyes to run. Just two strong legs and a heart.

So Joe ran a lot. He ran indoors on the "Y" track and—when he could get someone to go with him—he ran outdoors. Finally, a friend of his—Dr. Vincent Savino, a dentist—said to him one day: "Why don't you run in the Boston Marathon?"

Joe's heart jumped; so did his legs.

Why didn't he think of that? The Boston Marathon. That'd be like playing in the Super Bowl or maybe at Wimbledon or teeing up at the U.S. Open. The Boston Marathon was the World Series of running.

Dr. Savino told Joe he'd run with him. Together, they arrived at a scheme that would enable them to cover the 26 miles 385 yards of the Marathon. The good doctor would lead the way and Joe would simply hang on and follow.

They ran as an unofficial entry in 1972 but like so many schemes, this one would fail. Joe wanted to run too fast.

"We were somewhere in the middle of the pack," Pardo recalled. "I was a little nervous. I'd never run in a race before and I was afraid I'd get trampled once we got started."

The result was that once the gun went off and they got moving out of Hopkinton, Joe turned it on. Now it was Dr. Savino who had to hang on.

"We argued all the time we were out there," said Dr. Savino. "We were going to run nine-minute miles, which would get us in under four hours. That was plenty good enough for us. But here we were averaging seven minutes and forty seconds and it was killing me. I kept telling Joe to slow down. I told him, 'Hey, we're not in a one hundred-yard dash.'"

His adrenaline pumping—not to mention his legs—Joe Pardo could not slow down even if he had wanted to. Off he went by himself, leaving his friend behind. Joe Pardo's shorts became a living baton in the world's longest relay race. Runners would come along, grab the elastic band for a while, then pass it on to someone else.

Pardo ran with a doctor from the Bronx, two guys from Somerville, Massachusetts, a fellow from Trenton, and a Frenchman from Montreal. He went sailing through the hills of Newton, past Boston College and was well along Commonwealth Avenue when his right leg cramped up. He had to come to a halt and walk off the course.

Now he is standing there, alone. Nobody is aware that he is blind. He is just one more runner who packed it in.

"That was the lonesomest feeling in the world," he said. "I was out of the race and my leg hurt and I didn't know where the hell I was. And I didn't have a cent on me. I just stood there, wondering what was going to happen."

Along came a trolley and Dr. Savino was on it. He talked his way onto it. Now he saw Joe and got out.

Now they both stood around, wondering what to do. Neither had any money on them.

Finally, another trolley came along and the compassionate conductor took one look at them and said: "Come on, I'll give you a ride." They rode into Boston, Joe tired and wiser for his experience, Dr. Savino just tired.

Joe would run again, and he would finish. But he would not be so foolhardy as to think he could run the Boston Marathon into the ground. He treated it with respect, and even brought along a transistor radio to keep his mind off setting too fast a pace.

It was Leigh Montville of the *Boston Globe* who uncovered this story about Joe Pardo. I had heard of blind runners competing in the Boston Marathon but could not find anything about them in any of the files until I came across a clipping about a man named Alfred Ventrillo, who not only ran blind in the Boston Marathon but was doing it at the age of sixty-seven.

Alfred Ventrillo lives in Methuen, Massachusetts, a small town about thirty-five miles north of Boston. The moment I saw his name in the clipping, I knew I had to see him. I had to find out what motivates a man to run 26 miles 385 yards when he can't see a thing along the way.

I called Alfred Ventrillo on the phone and my heart sank the moment I heard his voice. He spoke very slowly . . . very shakily . . . and it was difficult understanding him.

But I knew I still had to meet him.

I found myself also speaking very slowly to him, saying, "Now, Alfred, I'll be out to see you tomorrow but I'll call you first from my hotel. It'll be in the morning. I'll call first. Do you understand?"

"Yes," he replied softly, "I understand."

That morning I was going to drive the Marathon course with Tommy Leonard, my bartender buddy. I called Alfred and told him I'd be out sometime in the afternoon, probably late afternoon.

"You got that?"

"Yes," he said. "I've got it."

Methuen is a dingy town, worn and weary from too many years on this earth. Everything seemed gray. Buildings were boarded up and the air was dusty from too much smoke belching from too many factories.

It was about 4:30 in the afternoon when I finally found Mystic Street. A man was standing on the porch of 24 Mystic Street. He was wearing dark glasses and was clad in pink pajamas and heavy boots.

As I cut the engine on the car and started to get out, his head moved ever so slightly, his ear cocked in my direction. "Joe, is that you?"

"Yeah, Alfred, it's me. The world's slowest runner is here."

At once his whole body seemed to relax. "Oh, good," he said. He had been waiting on that porch since nine o'clock in the morning, right after my call, a vigil of more than eight hours.

He felt his way along the wall and led the way into his apartment. Again my heart sank. It was dismal in here. All that was in the living room was a ragged chair and a musty sofa. No rug on the floor. In the kitchen, dishes and books and paper—and a typewriter—were piled on the table.

Alfred Ventrillo had one light on. It was a bright light and it was blazing in one corner of the living room. He had it turned up so that it was shining on a blood-red warm-up suit hanging from a coatrack. The white lettering on the front of the uniform read: "My Final Race Age 68 Blind."

Alfred Ventrillo had planned to make the 1976 Boston Marathon the final race of his life, but the fates had worked against him. A thief had broken into his apartment and poisoned his Seeing Eye dog, Goldie. And the doctors had found that Alfred was suffering from high blood pressure.

And so, on the morning of April 19, 1976—when they were lining up at the village green in Hopkinton—Alfred Ventrillo was at his doctor's office for a checkup. He didn't dare so much as turn on his radio for fear he would hear the words: "Boston Marathon."

Now he was smiling as he led the way into the kitchen. "Here, Joe," he was saying, "I know you've had a long trip. Have some tonic and cake before we talk."

On the table was a bottle of orange pop and a piece of cake with chocolate icing. The bottle was unopened. I touched it. It was warm.

"Maybe later, Alfred. Let's talk first. I've got a lot of things to ask you."

We spoke for about two hours. It was impossible to pin him down on names, dates and places. He has been legally blind since sometime in the late 1940s. His right eye is made of plastic. His left eye absorbs only a touch of light. If you place a sheet of white paper in front of him, he can see the whiteness. But that's all.

The rest of the time his vision is a blurry red—"like a flame," he said.

I disliked myself for doing it—and feel shameful to admit it now—but as we spoke I edged off to one side to see if Alfred would follow my movements. He didn't.

He told me that he ran the Marathon with the aid of a Y.M.C.A. director, who led the way by pinching the side of his shorts. The man was supposed to run only half the race and a colleague was supposed to pick them up and lead Alfred the rest of the way.

He sat there laughing. "I tricked him, though," he said. "I told him we only had a little ways to go. I told him we were almost there. So he stayed with me and he ran the whole distance himself."

Alfred told me about his beloved Goldie, how the thief broke into his apartment when he lived in Brockton and poisoned his dog. A chill ran through me when he described just lying in bed, afraid to breathe, fearful he would arouse the burglar and he might come in and attack him.

"I couldn't do anything but lay there," he said. "I was very scared. I didn't even want to move."

The painters had been in his apartment that afternoon. They had left the window open so that the apartment would get some air. That's how the thief made his way in.

And all he took was one album from Alfred Ventrillo's record collection, and Goldie's life.

"Goldie liked it where it was cool," said Alfred Ventrillo. "When they opened the window, that's where she went to sleep. When the burglar came in, he gave her something and she got very sick.

"We made a good team, Goldie and me. She didn't like my running but she put up with it. Every day we'd go down to the field and I'd run two hours and ten minutes. I'd leash her up to a special place and when there was just five minutes to go—and she knew it every time—she'd bark three times and I knew I was almost finished."

After the theft, Alfred Ventrillo's relatives moved him out of Brockton and into his apartment in Methuen, so he could be closer to his sister.

As we spoke, Alfred kept getting up and running his hand across the wall to where two picture frames were hanging. The frames contained typewritten letters and Alfred kept saying: "Please read these to me, Joe."

I kept driving for names, dates, places and races. Finally, he pleaded: 'Please, Joe, just read one of them.''

I took one down from the wall and read it aloud. This is what it said:

May 7, 1975

Alfred Ventrillo
24 Golden Circle
Brockton, Mass.

Dear Alfred:

I continue to be amazed at your athletic prowess in running the 1975 Boston Marathon. I thought your grand performance in the 1973 Marathon was a truly great accomplishment. But to make a comeback in 1975 is an even greater accomplishment. It demonstrates the determination and innate strength of your character.

Over the years you have trained and developed your body with Spartan discipline. You have also developed your spiritual life and indeed your entire life-style with equal discipline and determination.

It is because of your great spirit that you make this extraordinary victory over blindness such an important accomplishment. You deserve an abundance of praise and please add my name to the long list of your admirers.

Sincerely,
John F. Mungoven
Commissioner for the Blind
Commonwealth of Massachusetts

Alfred Ventrillo giggled as I read the letter. "See, Joe, see," he kept saying. "It's a good thing I wasn't a hockey player or I'd never get any letters like this."

18
Alas, Poor Erich

YOU DON'T SEE ERICH SEGAL around the Boston Marathon very much any more. In fact, you don't see him at all.

Alas, poor Erich made a sad mistake. He became too famous. Too rich. Too well known.

It is really too bad because in the innocent days of the 1950s, Erich Segal was what the Boston Marathon was all about. He was a plodder, a joyful plodder. A student at Harvard, he took part in this April ritual every year. It was a time to cleanse the soul and the body, a time to assert one's independence. Erich Segal would be out there, plodding along, No. 764 . . . or maybe it was No. 688 . . . and nobody paid much of a mind to him. He was part of the scenery, this magnificent montage of nameless runners who make this such a great event.

Erich liked it a lot better then, too. He could run in peace, at his own pace, and for his own reasons. He ran in fifteen Boston Marathons before he hit with *Love Story*, his syrup-sweet tale of love that captured the world's fancy and aroused critics around the globe.

Erich got trapped by too much fame. The more his book sold, the more his critics rapped him. The more the critics rapped him, the more defensive he became. Finally, he withdrew—not only from the Marathon but from society. For one whole year nobody could find him. He thought that time could be an ally. He felt if he stayed away from everyone—out of the glare of the public— he might be accepted again. He might be Erich Segal, No. 784, and he could trudge through the flat roads of Framingham, pass the girls at Wellesley, plow up the hills of Newton, and glide down to the finish line in Boston, his vigor restored, his faith renewed, his mind and body refreshed.

But they wouldn't let him alone. Whenever he ran, they looked for him—at every checkpoint and in between. They'd thrust his book before him, asking him to stop and autograph it. He didn't know what to do. If he ran on, they might mistake it for contempt. If he stopped, the other runners would glare at him in contempt. It was a race he could not win.

Coming through Wellesley—a spot he loved so dearly because Erich dearly loved the girls—they taunted him with signs and banners: "Male Chauvinist Pig—This Is Your Penance."

It hurt.

It hurt deep down. What had he done? Nothing more than realize the great American dream. He went from hopeful sophomore at Harvard to world-renowned author. But few liked his work—except the millions who bought his book and the millions who saw the movie. He was a success everywhere except among his colleagues and out on the winding roads of New England.

What's so sad is that Segal did love to run. You don't compete in seventeen Boston Marathons—each a torture of its own—without having a feeling for the sport. Erich felt deeply. But once he made it big, he was no longer a face in the crowd but a genuine celebrity, trying to cash in—many thought—on his newfound fame.

Segal ran in the 1971 Marathon and as he sat in the cafeteria at Big Pru, he sipped on his Gatorade and said: "I'm sick of the limelight. They thought I'd be sipping champagne from girls' slippers, but look!"—he held up the bottle of Gatorade—"I'm drinking this stuff from a girl's track shoe."

Say what you will about this man's literary prowess, there is no questioning his love of running. It's genuine.

He began running in his early days at Midwood High School in Brooklyn ("I wasn't dead last in every race") and continued

142

through his years at Harvard. He entered his first Boston Marathon in 1955.

"I was running for Harvard and the coach, Bill McCurdy, said one day: 'Segal, go out and run ten miles.' So I did. I was so unwinded when I finished that McCurdy said, 'Segal, you couldn't have run that fast.' I said, 'But I did.' That's when he told me I should try out for the Marathon."

Segal once finished fiftieth, a highly credible feat, and his best time was 2 hours 56 minutes 30 seconds, another credible feat. Nobody knew it then because he was Erich Segal, citizen; now they wish to forget it because he is Erich Segal, celebrity.

It is little wonder they have grown to dislike him. Envy is easily acquired. Not only could he speak Latin, but he could converse in Italian, French, Dutch, Spanish and some German. That, alone, was enough to put him high on a lot of jealousy lists.

Segal wrote the original draft for his astoundingly successful book in eight days of the Christmas holiday in 1968. It was written on seventy-seven typewritten blue-colored pages to distinguish it from his diverse other projects. A bachelor, a little guy of just 5-foot-6 and 135 pounds, with strong brown eyes and black, wiry hair (not exactly your Greek Adonis), Segal became wealthy almost overnight. Copies of his book were everywhere—at first, one million hard-cover and ten million paperback in the United States alone. It sold one million copies in France and Italy. In Japan, under the title *Love and Death*, it quickly sold 250,000 hard-cover copies, more than twice as many as most popular Japanese novels. Segal received $65,000 for writing the screenplay for the movie, But this was a mere pittance compared to the 10 percent he received out of the gross of $25 million in the first three months the movie was on the market. The clamor—and the glamour—was so great that he even had to quit his position as professor of classic culture and English literature at Yale. The students wanted to talk to him instead of listen to him.

It wasn't all suffering for Erich.

"I started taking out better girls. When I was a Midwood High, I was too shy to call the Junior Prom Queen and ask for a date. Now, lovely girls were sending me mash notes and the keys to their apartments. I've always liked the fleshpots, so that part of it was good."

The truth is, Segal could buy anything he wanted. He remembers walking into a shop on Fifth Avenue in New York City and admiring a $1,000 muskrat-lined raincoat. He tried it on and it fit perfectly.

Salesman: "Hey, aren't you Erich Segal, the *Love Story* guy?"

Segal: "Yes."

Salesman: "Will you be wearing that coat in public?"

Segal: "My dear man, I don't wear coats in private."

Salesman: "Just a minute. Don't go away. I have to go upstairs."

Moments later, after conferring with the store's bigwigs, the salesman returned with the happy news that Segal could have the coat at no cost. Free! One of the by-products of his fame was staring him right in the face. He felt elated—and a little deflated.

"I easily could have afforded that coat," he said. "Now it was mine—for zero—just because I was me."

Powerful stuff.

But sorrowful, too.

For dear Erich no longer runs in the Marathon. The purpose somehow is gone for him.

After his last Marathon a reporter asked him if he had a secret and impossible dream—this man who had acquired so much in life.

"Yes, I do," said Segal. "I want to win the Boston Marathon. Now it is a secret no longer. But it is impossible."

19

Spinning Their Wheels

THE FIRST TIME I ever saw the Boston Marathon I nearly got run down.

It was out in Hopkinton, on that quiet street just up from the village green, where they start the race.

They were all bunched together at the starting line. I was standing there with Ray Fitzgerald of the *Boston Globe*.

We knew this was going to be something—this mass of humanity rushing at us, thundering past us like a giant herd of buffalo.

"Let's time them."

It was no original idea. I'd heard all kinds of reports of how long it took them to get over the starting line. Two minutes. Three minutes. Five minutes. I suppose it depended on your vantage point—if you were out there in the middle of that pack or standing here alongside the street. Your pulse rate and heartbeat probably have a lot to do with the correct calculation.

The gun went off . . . and here they came, rumbling at first, moving slowly, then faster—and soon just a swirl of arms and legs and bodies and caps and legs and shirts and shorts and legs.

As they were streaming by, I stepped out to get a better look— especially at the gal who just went by—the one with the green snakes on the front of her blouse. The back of her blouse said: "Serpents of Temptation."

"See you in Boston!"

She turned and smiled and threw a kiss back. And it was then —in this moment of rapture—that I nearly got it.

Zzzzzzzzzzzz.

This guy went wheeling past me and just missed my toes by a matter of inches.

I couldn't believe it. Here were these thousands of guys and gals bouncing past us in what was still a blur of bodies and this guy is gunning down the side of the street in a wheelchair.

I mean he's giving it all he's got. He's pumping like mad—his body straining forward—keeping pace with everyone at his side.

Hell, he was going faster than most of them.

"Did you see that! Did you see that guy in the wheelchair! What's that all about?"

Ray, the old pro, merely smiled: "It's the Boston Marathon, isn't it?"

The guy was 23-year-old Bob Hall, a special education teacher from Belmont, Massachusetts. He had been crippled since the age of one, when he was stricken with polio. I hoped I would see him downtown, at the Pru, but never did. Will McDonough of the *Boston Globe* staff found him and did a story about him.

I'd heard of the "guy in the wheelchair" and mentioned it to one of the officials two days before the race. He half-sneered: "He's not part of the race—we don't count him."

I couldn't believe my ears. I'd have given him a number and maybe put a siren on his wheelchair, with flashing red lights, and a string of balloons trailing behind him. To go the distance in a wheelchair—down the hills, *wheeeeee!* But how about going up? How in the world do you push a wheelchair up a hill?

Anyway, Will McDonough is enough of a newspaperman to seek out Hall, and he discovered that Hall was the first person to go the 26 miles 385 yards without his feet ever touching the ground. They'd had another wheelchair competitor back in 1970—a Vietnam amputee named Gene Roberts—but he "ran" part of the course on his hands. In fact, he did about three miles on his hands, before finally finishing in his wheelchair.

"I'm really not an official entry," Hall told McDonough. "I can't be, because I can't run. But I talked to the Marathon officials and they said they'd let me get into the race."

It wasn't a gimmick with Hall. He was merely making the most of the hand that life had dealt him. He had entered the Wheelchair Marathon in Ohio and when he won that he immediately set his sights on Boston.

He worked out every day, testing himself on the hills of Newton.

"They were tough . . . no sense kidding about it," said Hall. "In the Wheelchair Marathon the race was run over flat ground. You didn't have to contend with any hills. I didn't want them to beat me in this race."

Hall finished in 2:58, ahead of almost half the field. He had aimed for three hours and beat his goal by two minutes. His mark may stand forever.

"My hands got a little sore because I had to do so much braking," he said. "I had to cut in and out of a lot of runners. But I had my fingers taped so the blisters wouldn't become a problem. It really went very well for me."

In high school Hall had to settle for being manager of the teams. He'd wheel his way around picking up sweat shirts and towels.

He wanted more. He wanted to "run."

"I read somewhere that the record for a mile in the wheelchair was something like six minutes and twenty-four seconds. I told myself if I could do that, I'd take on The Boston."

Hall went to Billy Squires, the great former distance runner and track coach at Boston State. He told him what he wanted to do and Squires encouraged him.

"He told me how to run," smiled Hall. "He knew I was sincere and so he told me just how I'd have to train for it."

When Gene Roberts "ran" the course in his wheelchair in 1970, it took him six hours and seven minutes. That's because he went part of the way on his hands—"hand-jockeying," he called it.

Roberts lost his legs after being shot up in a search-and-destroy mission in Vietnam on May 26, 1966. He was hit by a 105-mm howitzer, which killed five members in his company.

One leg was amputated immediately. The other had to be amputated later on. Roberts considered himself very lucky, not the least bit resentful of his fate.

Roberts "ran" with the inscription "Praise the Lord" on his shirt.

That's what he sang as he turned the corner and came down the hill to the finish line.

"I guess I felt I owed God something for letting me live," he said. "But if it wasn't for those people out there, I never would have finished."

Roberts drove to Boston with his brother Jim and a friend. For two nights the three of them slept in the car.

Roberts started ahead of the official noon starting time so that he wouldn't block the way for others. He picked up friends and supporters all along the way. Three Boston College students joined him near Cleveland Circle and walked at his side for a while. But his pace was too fast and he soon left them behind.

"I wondered what people might think of me," said Roberts, who didn't want to seem like a grandstander, even when he was standing on his hands. "I finally decided I had to do this thing because you don't see too many people praising the Lord. I feel the best way to live is to be an athlete and to love God."

Roberts, married and the father of a girl, then broke into a wide smile.

"Someday," he said, "I'd like to swim the English Channel."

20

Man's Worst Friend

THE AMAZING THING about those old archenemies—runners vs. dogs—is that there are so many runners in the Boston Marathon and so few dogs.

You'd think the mutts would have a field day with four thousand legs bouncing past them in an almost endless procession. That's like living in T-bone heaven. But the people who live along the route of this race that winds through the New England countryside are pretty considerate of the runners. Not only do they provide cups of water and ice cubes and orange slices but they learned long ago that Patriots' Day means something else: That's the day you put the leash on Fido on the morning of the race. Or else Fido goes bozo, and so do the runners.

Dogs are a very real menace to runners, especially distance runners who are usually out by themselves trotting down some country road or through the streets of the neighborhood. There isn't a distance runner alive—man or woman—who hasn't experienced the chilling fear of having an angry dog chasing after him or her.

It is a dog's instinct to chase after a moving object. They can't help but protect their property. Many dogs are basically cowards, but if they see something running away from them, it bolsters their confidence and brings out the spirit of the hunt. That's why you never see a dog lying in ambush and springing on a runner as he approaches. The dog is always in pursuit.

So it was left to Tom Osler, writing in *The Runners' World*, to offer some logical (but hard to pull off) ways of handling pursuing dogs. You can throw stones at them or hit them with baseball bats or even beat them with chains or spray them with chemicals. But who carries such weapons in a run through the streets or out in the woods? The victim is usually empty-handed and is usually taken by surprise.

So Osler offers these tips:

• Don't try to run away. This only provokes the dog, and you can't outrun anything faster than a Basset hound. If a dog makes a menacing gesture at you, slow down, walk or stop. Don't let him get behind you.

• Take the offensive. Shout at the dog. Yell "halt," "stop" or more original epithets. Or simply answer in kind with growls and barks of your own. Anything to frighten the animal. Noise inspires fear, which stops most attacks.

• If noise doesn't work, try a weapon. Reach down for a stick, stone or can, and threaten him with it. The simple act of reaching for an instrument usually causes a dog to lose heart. The dog has learned before that man is far more dangerous with something in his hand.

Except for an inevitable stray, the Boston Marathon has become a very safe race as far as the dog menace is concerned. That's because of what happened to young John Kelley in 1961 when he was bowled over by a black mongrel and it probably cost him his chance to win. He finished only twenty yards behind the winner. Had he not been bowled over—costing him his running rhythm as well as valuable time—he might have taken the title. As it was, he just missed by twenty-five seconds.

The old race has had a few other incidents involving dogs. The immortal Clarence H. DeMar once drop-kicked a persistent Pomeranian the width of Main Street in Natick. The late Pat Dengis paused to hurl a handful of rocks at an unrelenting hound. Yun Bok Suh, at 5-foot-1 the smallest man ever to win the Marathon, was knocked down by a dog at the twenty-mile mark before getting up and going on to victory. Even the irascible Jock Semple got nipped in his running days and the rumor is that he bit the dog back.

But it was not until the Kelley incident in 1961 that any real steps were taken to curtail the dog menace. The Massachusetts S.P.C.A. stepped into the picture and offered, free of charge, a Dog Control Service. The offer was accepted by the late Walter A. Brown, the man who moderated the Marathon. Three radio-controlled cars were set up, each with loudspeakers, and these would precede the runners along the route and advise dog owners to restrain their animals. They even offered free leashes.

The Kelley incident, while an unfortunate one for the American star, produced one of the real shows of sportsmanship in the Marathon.

On a wintry, windy April 19, amid flurries of light snow, Kelley hooked up in a tremendous battle with a pink-skinned Finn named Eino Oksanen and a freshman from McNeese State College in Louisiana named Jim Norris. They were running as tightly as if covered by Saran Wrap when they were broken apart at the sixteen-mile mark. For more than ten miles the group had been paced by the mongrel who now suddenly swerved from the left side of the road into the path of the runners. Oksanen jumped to avoid him, but the dog hit Kelley full across the legs and he went down violently. For an instant it looked as if the race was over for Kelley. He lay there, flat against the ground, momentarily stunned. Norris, who also avoided the dog, stopped abruptly and came back to help Kelley to his feet.

"It happened so fast that I hardly had time to think," Norris said after the race. "He looked as if he was down to stay, and he'd been running such a good race. So I grabbed him and shouted, 'Get up!' It snapped him out of the shock and we started running right away."

But the damage had been done. Not only had Oksanen sprinted off into the lead, but Kelley and Norris had lost that strong, steady, almost trancelike tempo that drives distance runners on, far beyond their own capacity. Once this momentum is broken, it is almost never regained. The effort of stopping and returning and lifting Kelley's deadweight had been doubly severe on Norris, since he had already been wincing from a stitch in his side. They took off in game pursuit of the Finn, and though Kelley passed him once, he was not strong enough to put him away.

21

"Doctor, Can You Give Me a Hand With My Feet?"

THE F.B.I. ALWAYS GETS ITS MAN, right? Isn't that what Efrem Zimbalist, Jr., taught us for years on Sunday nights?

There was this F.B.I. agent running in the Boston Marathon about six or seven years ago. He wasn't shadowing anyone. He was just trying to keep up with himself, as it were.

The poor guy was having all sorts of problems. It was warm and his throat was dry and the road was hard and his legs were getting crampy.

And then—worst of all—one of his shoelaces snapped.

That's pretty embarrassing—to be a runner in the world's greatest footrace and have a shoelace break. Who brings along extra shoelaces? So our man—ever ingenious—merely stopped and took some tape out of his pocket (he remembered to bring that along) and taped the shoe to his foot. Within a few miles the tape began cutting into his skin and the blood flowed so profusely that his whole foot became a mass of red blisters.

"That was one of the stranger cases we've had over the years," said Dr. Thomas Connolly, one of the many physicians who donate their time to the runners on April 19.

Now that the Boston Marathon has grown to such immense

proportions, more doctors than ever are needed to minister to the runners when they come in, drawn and pale—almost all ashen gray—to seek aid at the finish.

Dr. Connolly has been at it for eighteen years and remembers the old days when the runners finished in front of the Lenox Hotel and were taken care of in the tiny basement classrooms of an old journalism school.

Now they work in the wide-open spaces of the Prudential garage —but the scene is still the same: It looks like the Battle of Bull Run and these are the losers.

"They come in with those empty expressions on their faces . . . it's amazing how they all look alike," Dr. Connolly says. "They're in like a state of shock—well, that's exactly what it is for some of them. They've been out there pounding away so long that not much blood is getting to the brain."

So the good doctor comforts them—let's them know there is someone to care for them—and then wraps them in blankets and puts them on cots (or on the floor if all the cots are filled) and props their feet in the air.

The surprising thing is that nothing is ever seriously wrong with these runners. Dr. Connolly can remember only two times when they had to call an ambulance in his eighteen years on the job—and both were for precautionary measures and not because of any emergency.

Dr. Connolly is not your ordinary physician. You'll find him down in the basement of the Pru at six and seven o'clock in the evening—as long as there are runners finishing and someone needs his help. Some doctors will stay around just for the first few finishers, sharing in their glory and maybe getting their pictures in the papers. Happily, these are few in number. Most are like Dr. Connolly, dedicated men who are strangely drawn to this race.

"I keep saying I'm not going to come back any more, but I always think there might be somebody who needs my help," says Dr. Connolly. Like the blind man he saw standing on a street corner at about seven o'clock one night. He had run the race and now was trying to get a ride to the bus depot so he could return to his home. Dr. Connolly took him to the depot and never bothered to get his name. That wasn't important. He needed help and that was that.

"The good runners don't need any help. They're always in good

153

shape. I see them come in here to pick up their gear and they're not even breathing hard. But it's those other fellows, the plodders, who need us."

The doctors number between ten and twenty at any given race. They will be assisted by nurses and other volunteers. They do a remarkable job—offering understanding as well as medical aid.

"Sometimes all they need is a word to tell them they're okay," Dr. Connolly relates. Sometimes they need to have almost all the skin cut from the bottoms of their feet—such is the great problem with blisters.

The curious thing is that the runners never complain of sore feet when they are running.

"It's like a boxer, after he gets hit for the second time. He doesn't feel the pain any more. When they're out there running, they all but beat the blood out of their feet."

The legs cause the most pain, because the blood is still circulating in the legs and the runners can feel the pain.

"The greatest problem is getting blood through the system," the doctor says. "When the physicians examined Clarence H. DeMar, they found his aorta was as large as a thumb. That was one reason why he was such a great runner. The blood flowed smoothly through his system."

In other words, the feet don't start hurting until the runners stop running. That's when the blood gets back into them. Then they hurt a lot.

"If Ponce de León could have found a way to keep the blood flowing to the feet and to the brain, he would have indeed discovered the 'Fountain of Youth,'" tells Dr. Connolly.

When Dr. Connolly comes across a runner who seems out of it, he'll ask him a few simple questions to test his mental reflexes.

"Are you in the Science Museum?" he may say.

If the runner tells him, no, he's in the basement at the Pru, he's okay. But if he says he's on the Staten Island Ferry, it's time to give him immediate attention.

"It's so strange . . . they're appreciative of any thing we do for them," Dr. Connolly remembers with a smile. "Even if we just move them, they appreciate it."

One of the things that bothered Dr. Connolly for years was the shortage of blankets. It is important to keep a runner warm after absorbing such punishment.

"I found myself taking one soggy blanket off one runner and throwing it across another," he says. "That was really bad."

Dr. Connolly suggested the use of disposable blankets and these are now in use, courtesy of the Prudential Insurance Company.

While no serious ailments have ever developed in Dr. Connolly's years on the job, it is not a pleasant scene in the ward at the finish line. He thought his kids might be interested in seeing just what he does at the Boston Marathon. The one year he brought them with him, they got sick to their stomachs.

Most of the runners just need to relax—to let their muscles return to normal. Dr. Connolly says the pain can be quite severe for a while. In time, though, they are usually able to make their way around.

The two big concerns—the main dangers—are heat exhaustion and heatstroke. One can be harmful, the other deadly. Billy Squires, a professor of health science and track coach at Boston State College, passes along these tips:

Symptoms of heat exhaustion:
Extremely heavy sweating; weak or rapid pulse; cold, clammy skin; shallow breathing, pale face.
Treatment:
Move patient to a cool place and treat for shock; lower the head and, if possible, raise the feet and legs; use ice or cold packs on the forehead, neck and wrists; massage the arms and legs slightly. Call a physician.
Symptoms of heatstroke:
No sweating; a strong, rapid pulse; extremely high temperature, from 106 to 112 degrees; flushed or grayish skin; labored breathing; could collapse, lose consciousness or go into convulsions.
Treatment:
Move patient to cooler place; keep the head and upper part of body slightly elevated; do not lower the head; wrap the patient in cold, wet sheets or cool in the best way possible. Call a physician immediately. Heatstroke is a serious ailment that presents complications far beyond the abilities of first aid.

Luckily, many doctors are interested in running. Some even run the race themselves, then attend to the runners after they finish. Once, to demonstrate the advantages of running, a team of seven heart patients from Toronto (with twelve heart attacks among them)

155

ran as a unit in the Boston Marathon. All of them finished and said they "felt just great."

And now—of course—the debate rages as to whether men or women are physically more capable of running marathon distances.

Dr. Joan Ullyot, a marathoner herself and a physiologist from San Francisco, maintains that women are better equipped to meet the demands of going 26 miles 385 yards.

She explains that the body uses up glycogen—"muscle starch"— during an extended run: "Women seem to be able to burn fat better than men. After twenty miles or so, when the glycogen is used up, men tend to 'hit the wall.' They have to go the last few miles on sheer guts. Women don't seem to hit the wall, because they convert from glycogen to fat more easily, more naturally."

Dr. Ernest Jokl, a physiologist from Lexington, Kentucky, has worked with Dr. Ullyot and calls her theory "a lot of rubbish."

So there you are.

Now that women are here to stay as bona fide competitors in the Boston Marathon, we offer—at no extra charge—the following tips on how to keep their feet in shape, courtesy of two Boston podiatrists, Dr. Marguerite F. Cobb and Dr. Amy B. Katzew:

• Don't flop around the house in rundown old slippers or distorted shoes. When you're working around the house, wear sensible shoes with medium to low heels for support.

• Don't do any self-surgery—on bunions, blisters, corns or whatever. This is particularly important for diabetes sufferers and also older folks who can't see too well and whose hands might be a little shaky.

• Don't wear shoes that cause undue pressure on any part of the foot.

• Stay away from sling-backs or backless shoes if the only way you can keep them on is by gripping excessively with your toes. This causes harmful pressures.

• Make sure your pantyhose or stockings do not bind your feet.

• Don't wear restricting garters—again this is particularly applicable to older women since it affects the circulation.

• For the same reason, avoid tight girdles.

• Don't make a habit of sitting wih your legs crossed. This is another way to restrict circulation.

• Don't walk around in bare feet. You run the risk of infection. If you feel like flinging off your shoes, do it on your own carpet at home—and even then it's wiser to keep your stockings on.

• Don't bathe your feet in either extremely hot or cold water. Use tepid.

22
And the Last Shall Be First

ONE OF THE MANY CHARMS of the Boston Marathon is that it produces all sorts of heroes.

The guy who wins.

The gal who wins.

Everyone who finishes.

And that poor lost soul who, at about six or seven o'clock in the evening, after everyone else has gone home and workmen are taking down the bunting and sweeping up the trash, all but stumbles across the line in last place.

For every first-place runner in the eighty Boston Marathons, there has been a last-place runner. Only sometimes we don't know his name. Sometimes we don't know when he finishes. And we don't even know why he finishes—except for some drive deep within him that keeps him going long after everyone has given up on him.

He's a hero, too.

The records are sketchy on last-place finishes because who wants to stand out there that long—sometimes in the rain, sometimes in the sleet, sometimes after a terribly hot and humid day—and watch some forlorn figure cross the line at six or seven o'clock in the evening. There are deadlines to be met, dinners to be cooked. Who has such time for such foolishness?

Happily, somebody cares enough to stay out there—usually an enterprising journalist, one with imagination or, perhaps, even with compassion.

Take 1974. It was shortly after six o'clock when Dr. Elias Shemin of Pleasantville New York, came trudging across the line, winner of last place.

"I feel terrible," said the good doctor. He hadn't qualified, but he decided to go the 26 miles 385 yards anyway. "I keep telling my patients to jog and so I thought I'd take my own advice. Now, I don't know what to tell them."

Dr. Shemin sat down on the curb. It had been a long and weary journey. He stopped once along the way—in Wellesley—to buy a new pair of sneakers. Another time, he didn't know where—he stopped in at a party and sat down and had some soda pop and chips for himself.

Dr. Shemin was a sorrowful figure, and yet there was glory in his deed, for how many had fallen and could not rise along the way. They go down on the hills of Newton, they collapse at Auburndale—sometimes they go out with a cramp or a sudden stitch in their side before they are but a mile down the road. It is a lot easier to live with sore feet than the knowledge that you had to quit. Hal Higdon can tell you about quitting.

Higdon is the best writer-runner who has ever competed in the Boston Marathon. He has finished well and written well. He has written a book on marathon running with a special emphasis on the Boston Marathon.

"You feel foolish when you have to quit," says Higdon. "It's like the whole world is looking at you. You go into the locker room and everyone's happy. When they ask you how you did, and you have to say you quit, you can't live with yourself.

"I still think about races I dropped out of ten years ago. Now I wish I had crawled the rest of the way on my hands and knees. It is difficult to live with the fact you've quit. It's like having a prison record."

Some of the officials of the race have no time, or patience, for the Dr. Shemins. That's too bad. They are missing an essential point of this race—maybe its very essence. Jock Semple merely shakes his head and says: "I kin walk this course faster than some of 'em can run it."

Maybe so. It takes some of us longer than others to conquer ourselves. Some of us never make it, not in an entire lifetime. But a Dr. Shemin has done it at least once, and he has tangible evidence, even if the proof rests only in his heart.

Personally, I'd give the last guy in a trophy, maybe a can of baked beans, or anything to commemorate his feat in the Boston Marathon. Why not? In the Port Huron-to-Mackinac sailboat race, they treat the last boat in with honor—with a special award for perseverance. Maybe it's only a jar of pickles—for being the "Pickle Boat"—but it is given with warmth, sincerity, affection, admiration —and a little bit of humor, which should also be a part of this race.

It just seems that somebody like Leo Lee of Brookline ought to get some recognition for his wondrous deed of going the full distance, even if he was last, even if it took him six hours and twenty-five minutes. He didn't quit, and that should count for something.

Lee was last across the line in 1966. The sun was fading when he came in, but he came in smiling. That's amazing. No tumultuous cheers, no garland of roses for this slim Japanese-born runner. He was greeted only by the pigeons and a few stares of the curious walking in front of Prudential Center.

There should be a place—even if it's last place—for the nebbishes who give it everything but never come close to the winner's circle—the guys who go down the wrong streets or get caught up in the traffic in Kenmore Square or get stopped for jaywalking.

Poor Leo Lee. He couldn't even claim a clear-cut defeat. Long after the last official had left and Lee came trotting home, a gang of New Jersey high school students were claiming that their man, Alan Berman, was to be the last one in. "Just wait. Alan's out on the course somewhere. He'll be here any minute."

But Alan Berman never showed. He was listed among the missing in action.

Lee, just eighteen, went home not knowing if he was or if he wasn't last. Somebody ought to stay around and make these things official.

Lee ran in the blue and yellow colors of the Massachusetts College of Art where he was a freshman. For a while these colors were obscured by a shirt given to him by a concerned laundry truck driver.

The driver saw Lee plodding along and stopped his truck.

"You okay?" he asked.

"Yes, but I'm a little cold," said Lee.

The driver then gave him a heavy shirt to wear.

Lee understood the impact of his feat. He said he credited his loss to a lack of training. "I only trained for seven weeks, a few miles a day," he said.

The last-place finisher in 1972 was a gentleman named Jake Brederson of Attleboro, Massachussets. When he crossed the line at 6:40 P.M., he let out a cry of joy. He was a speed walker from the North Medford Club and walked the entire distance. It was the third time he'd walked the course. He ran it nine other times and finished six of his runs. Walking, he said, was easier.

Thirty-four-year-old Brederson, the father of three, did not seem embarrassed to be last across the line.

"I guess I did it to encourage my kids," he said. "My father was a runner for twenty years and he first interested me and my two brothers in running. He never pushed us, though.

"Usually I walk thirty or forty miles a week with one long walk a month to build up my endurance."

The longest he'd ever walked was fifty miles to the Brockton Fairgrounds and back. And what did he get out of going the full distance in the Boston Marathon?

"I got a few blisters, for one thing," he smiled. "But my real reward is that I'll be able to tell my grandchildren that I was in twelve Marathons. Or maybe I'll tell them it was twenty."

And, finally there is Charles B. Timpany, forty-four, the last-place finisher in 1954. He had to soak his tired feet after going the whole distance but was bubbling with joy because he got to run alongside the great Clarence H. DeMar.

Only for a short way, mind you. But it was like batting behind Ruth and Gehrig on the '27 Yankees.

"It was some thrill just to be at his side," recalls Timpany. "He was the greatest Marathoner of them all."

DeMar was sixty-six at the time and winding down his fabulous career in the Boston race.

"We exchanged a few words, but mostly it was just watching

that crowd—the reception they gave him all along the way . . . or as long as I could stay up with him. I seen a lot of these races and I can't remember one when I didn't learn something just from watching Mr. DeMar," says Timpany.

He had always wanted to be an athlete. He had tried almost all the team sports as a kid—baseball, football and hockey. But it was almost impossible for Timpany to make it because of his extreme nearsightedness.

But he could run. He had found that out early in life and had made the most of it. He was not always a plodder. He once finished thirty-eighth in the Boston Marathon with a time of 3 hours 9 minutes 20 seconds. That was in 1942.

How about it, Jock? One can of beans, maybe with a blue and gold ribbon on it, the colors of the old B.A.A. I'll throw in the brown bread.

23

Marathon Champions

YEAR	NAME	AGE	HT.	WT.	OCCUPATION
1897	John J. McDermott, New York City	25	5-6	124	unknown
1898	Ronald J. McDonald, Cambridge, Mass.	22	5-7	142	student
1899	Lawrence Brignolia, Cambridge, Mass.	23	5-10	173	blacksmith
1900	James J. Caffrey, Hamilton, Ont.	23	5-8	128	carpenter
1901	James J. Caffrey, Hamilton, Ont.	24	5-8	130	carpenter
1902	Sammy Mellor, Yonkers, N.Y.	23	5-6	128	unknown
1903	John C. Lorden, Cambridge, Mass.	28	5-7	136	unknown
1904	Michael Spring, New York City	21	5-6	118	clerk
1905	Fred Lorz, New York City	25	5-8	153	unknown
1906	Timothy Ford, Cambridge, Mass.	18	5-6	113	plumber
1907	Tom Longboat, Hamilton, Ont.	19	5-8	146	farmer
1908	Thomas Morrissey, New York City	20	5-7	133	unknown
1909	Henri Renaud, Nashua, N.H.	19	5-8	143	mill hand
1910	Fred Cameron, Nova Scotia	23	5-3	120	clerk
1911	Clarence H. DeMar, Melrose, Mass.	21	5-8	127	printer
1912	Mike Ryan, New York City	23	5-8	132	unknown
1913	Fritz Carlson, Minneapolis	29	5-7	142	lumberman
1914	James Duffy, Hamilton, Ont.	24	5-8	145	stonecutter
1915	Edouard Fabre, Montreal	28	5-7	147	steelworker

1916	Arthur Roth, Roxbury, Mass.	23	5-6	120 draftsman
1917	Bill Kennedy, Port Chester, N.Y.	35	5-7	135 bricklayer
1918	no race			
1919	Carl Linder, Quincy, Mass.	29	5-9	147 shipyard worker
1920	Peter Trivoulidas, New York City	29	5-6	132 busboy
1921	Frank Zuna, Newark, N.J.	28	5-9	151 plumber
1922	Clarence H. DeMar, Melrose, Mass.	32	5-8	137 printer
1923	Clarence H. DeMar, Melrose, Mass.	33	5-8	137 printer
1924	Clarence H. DeMar, Melrose, Mass.	34	5-8	137 printer
1925	Charles Mellor, Chicago	31	5-9	145 freight handler
1926	John C. Miles, Nova Scotia	19	5-7	133 delivery clerk
1927	Clarence H. DeMar, Melrose, Mass.	38	5-8	140 printer
1928	Clarence H. DeMar, Melrose, Mass.	39	5-8	140 printer
1929	John C. Miles, Hamilton, Ont.	22	5-7	136 clerk
1930	Clarence H. DeMar, Melrose, Mass.	41	5-8	142 teacher
1931	James Henigan, Medford, Mass.	38	5-7	136 milkman
1932	Paul de Bruyn, Germany	24	5-9	149 fireman
1933	Leslie Pawson, Pawtucket, R.I.	29	5-8	138 mill weaver
1934	Dave Komonen, Ontario	35	5-6	131 cobbler
1935	John A. Kelley, Arlington, Mass.	27	5-6	124 florist
1936	Ellison M. (Tarzan) Brown, Alton, R.I.	22	5-7	139 stonemason
1937	Walter Young, Quebec	24	5-11	145 unemployed
1938	Leslie Pawson, Pawtucket, R.I.	34	5-9	141 recreation worker
1939	Ellison M. (Tarzan) Brown, Alton, R.I.	25	5-7	138 unemployed
1940	Gerard Cote, Quebec	26	5-6	133 newsboy
1941	Leslie Pawson, Pawtucket, R.I.	37	5-9	143 recreation worker
1942	Bernard Joseph Smith, Medford, Mass.	27	6-2	160 milkman
1943	Gerard Cote, Quebec	29	5-6	135 soldier
1944	Gerard Cote, Quebec	30	5-6	135 soldier
1945	John A. Kelley, Arlington, Mass.	37	5-6	123 soldier
1946	Stylianos Kyriakides, Greece	36	5-7	134 bill collector
1947	Yun Bok Suh, Korea	24	5-1	115 student
1948	Gerard Cote, Quebec	34	5-6	135 distributor
1949	Karl Gosta Leandersson, Sweden	31	5-10	139 woodsman
1950	Kee Yong Ham, Korea	19	5-6	128 student
1951	Shigeki Tanaka, Japan	19	5-5	120 student
1952	Doroteo Flores, Guatemala	30	5-7	131 mill hand
1953	Keizo Yamada, Japan	24	5-2	108 clerk
1954	Veikko Karvonen, Finland	28	5-6	124 postal clerk
1955	Hideo Hamamura, Japan	25	5-7	132 clerk
1956	Antti Viskari, Finland	27	5-7	134 soldier
1957	John J. Kelley, Groton, Conn.	26	5-6	128 teacher
1958	Franjo Mihalic, Yugoslavia	36	5-7	125 printer
1959	Eino Oksanen, Finland	27	5-7	154 detective

1960	Paavo Kotila, Finland	32	5-7	140	farmer
1961	Eino Oksanen, Finland	29	5-7	154	detective
1962	Eino Oksanen, Finland	30	5-7	154	detective
1963	Aurele Vandendriessche, Belgium	28	5-7	132	bookkeeper
1964	Aurele Vandendriessche, Belgium	29	5-7	132	bookkeeper
1965	Morio Shigematsu, Japan	24	5-4	128	student
1966	Kenji Kimihara, Japan	25	5-5	130	clerk
1967	David McKenzie, New Zealand	24	5-4	123	printer
1968	Ambrose Burfoot, Groton, Conn.	21	6-0	140	student
1969	Yoshiaki Unetani, Japan	24	5-9	140	student
1970	Ron Hill, Great Britain	31	5-7	126	chemist
1971	Alvaro Mejia, Colombia	30	5-10	145	unemployed
1972	Olavi Suomalainen, Finland	25	5-7	126	student
1973	Jon Anderson, Eugene, Ore.	23	6-3	160	dishwasher
1974	Neil Cusack, Ireland	22	5-8	138	student
1975	Will Rodgers, Boston	27	5-9	130	student
1976	Jack Fultz, Franklin, Pa.	27	5-9	148	student

(Distance: 24½ miles)

1897

Winner: JOHN J. McDERMOTT, New York City. Time: 2h 55m 10s.

The first B.A.A. Marathon nearly ended in disaster when the winner ran into the middle of a funeral procession and stalled two of the newfangled electric cars. The mishap occurred on Massachusetts Avenue and created quite a stir in the funeral procession.

There were fifteen starters (six of them New Yorkers) in this inaugural race and John McDermott was the big favorite. During the previous October he had won the only marathon ever held on American soil—a test from Stamford, Connecticut, to Columbus Circle in New York City—and he was expected to repeat his victory. He did.

Despite the mixup with the funeral procession, McDermott was so far ahead of the field that he walked three times in the final ten miles and still won by seven minutes over his nearest rival.

1898

Winner: RONALD J. McDONALD, Cambridge, Mass. Time: 2h 42m.

Ronald McDonald—no hamburger—won the second Boston Marathon with a whirlwind finish, cutting thirteen minutes ten seconds off J. J. McDermott's time in the first race and leaving his closest competitor, New Yorker Hamilton Gray, gasping for air.

Gray, the New York cross-country champion, had raced himself into the road in the inaugural race and now he seemed to have this second race won when McDonald came on with his rush over the hills. Again Gray faded, losing a seven hundred-yard lead, and McDonald caught his man in Brookline and won by three minutes. The twenty-two-year-old Boston College student blazed the way in a pair of bicycle shoes.

1899

Winner: LAWRENCE BRIGNOLIA, Cambridge, Mass. Time: 2h 54m 38s.

The day was raw with a gusty eastern gale buffeting the course. But Lawrence Brignolia, a powerful blacksmith, was equal to the task.

In fact, he won even though a sudden gust caused him to step on a stone and fall. Brignolia sat on a curb for three minutes to regain his composure and his breath and still went on to win by three minutes. At 173 pounds, he is the heaviest man ever to win the race.

1900

Winner: JAMES J. CAFFREY, Hamilton, Ont. Time: 2h 39m 44s.

The Canadians entered the race for the first time and promptly made a shambles of the event with a 1-2-3 finish of Jim Caffrey, Bill Sherring and Frank Hughson. They were so eager that they caused the only false start in Marathon history. The field was called back when John Barnard of Canada jumped the gun.

Betting was heavy between Canadian and American followers and "bad blood" developed as a result of this race. Sherring held the lead for fifteen miles before he sat down on the grass to rest and Caffrey went right by him, never to be caught.

1901

Winner: JAMES J. CAFFREY, Hamilton, Ont. Time: 2h 29m 23s.

The Canadians were back again and, at twenty-four, Jim Caffrey became the first repeater in the B.A.A. race. He did it this time by bringing along his own competition—a Mohawk Indian named Bill Davis, who finished second.

The race was marred by a tinge of scandal when Ronald McDonald, the 1898 champion, collapsed at Cleveland Circle and rumors were rampant that he had been drugged. One doctor claimed the sponge

McDonald used to wipe his perspiring face contained chloroform, but the charge was never substantiated.

This race marked the entry of the first foreign runner—John Vrazanis of Greece. He was forced to drop out with blisters.

1902

Winner: SAMMY MELLOR, Yonkers, N.Y. Time: 2h 43m 12s.

Jim Caffrey, the tough Canadian, tried to make it three in a row but was stricken with dysentery before the race and—pale and weak—was persuaded by friends to withdraw from the contest after getting dressed in Ashland.

That made it an easy matter for tiny Sammy Mellor (just 5-foot-6, 128 pounds) to romp home the victor. Probably the most amazing feat is that a sixteen-year-old high school boy—Charlie Moody of Brighton High—finished fourth in 3h 03m 47s. This was before the age limit of eighteen years was established.

1903

Winner: JOHN C. LORDEN, Cambridge, Mass. Time: 2h 41m 29s.

This one figured to be a dogfight between Jim Caffrey, the two-time winner of 1900 and 1901, and little Sammy Mellor, the 1902 winner. And it was—for seventeen miles. The lead changed nine times between the two leaders, who also exchanged caustic remarks and insults on their run to the hills of Newton.

Then both men faltered. Caffrey withdrew with leg cramps and Mellor simply pooped out and was forced to walk. John Lorden, who had been plagued by leg cramps himself and also thought of quitting, suddenly got it together and came on to win by one of the biggest margins in Marathon history—almost six minutes—over the forlorn Mellor.

1904

Winner: MICHAEL SPRING, New York City. Time: 2h 38m 04s.

Poor Sammy Mellor. Once again he was doomed to failure, this time fading in the homestretch after setting a fast pace throughout most of the race.

Little Sammy was passed by five runners, led by Mike Spring, a twenty-year-old clerk. It turned out to be a significant victory for Spring, since the No. 2 man, Tom Hicks, went on to take the Olympic marathon title in St. Louis.

1905

Winner: FRED LORZ, New York City. Time: 2h 28m 25s.

This was a race of redemption, for Fred Lorz had been accused of "cheating" in the 1904 Olympic marathon in St. Louis for accepting a ride in an auto. The charge weighed heavily on Lorz's mind, until, out of sheer torment, he all but ran himself into exhaustion to win the Boston event.

Lorz's feet were blistered and bleeding at the end, and he collided with his own bicycle attendant and took a bad spill just at the finish line.

And poor little Sammy Mellor—he pooped out again with five miles to go and never finished.

1906

Winner: TIMOTHY FORD, Cambridge, Mass. Time: 2h 45m 45s.

The kids took over in the tenth race as eighteen-year-old Tim Ford became the youngest runner ever to win the Marathon—and by one of the slimmest margins in any marathon anywhere—just six seconds over Dave Kneeland of Roxbury.

Adding to the strange situation was the fact that Ford was a late entry—at first being rejected because he had submitted no entry. But the cocky runner talked his way into the race and ran wearing a golfing cap and chewing on a quill—not bad for a 113-pounder.

Sammy Mellor? He was among the leaders before saying bye-bye at the thirteen-mile mark.

1907

Winner: TOM LONGBOAT, Hamilton, Ont. Time: 2h 24m 24s.

This race should be remembered as the only time a freight train helped to decide the outcome of a marathon. Tom Longboat, nineteen, an Indian, was making his only Boston appearance and he set a hot early pace with Boston's red-haired James Lee.

It was a wise decision—for a freight train was to block the crossing path in South Framingham and only nine runners got by. The others had to stand around and wait until the train chugged out of the way.

Longboat also survived sleet and a driving rain to run the fastest Boston on record—an amazing accomplishment since he was still training on rocky roads out in the countryside.

1908

Winner: THOMAS MORRISSEY, New York City. Time: 2h 24m 43s.

It was another miserable day—but a good one for running. The sky was bleak and a spitting snow pelted the runners.

It was just what Tom Morrissey and John Hayes, who would go on to win the Olympic title in London, needed to put on a great duel. Tom Morrissey's superior condition at the moment finally prevailed and he beat Hayes over the line by twenty-one seconds. Only two minutes separated the first five finishers.

1909

Winner: HENRI RENAUD, Nashua, N.H. Time: 2h 53m 36s.

Now the old race turned into an inferno. It was a blistering 97 degrees, with the broiling sun leaving pools of melted tar and heat-stricken runners all over the road. The race pulled its biggest turnout yet—164 hopefuls. Of the 164, 91 fell by the wayside. Nine men held the lead through the first twenty miles—only to see all nine drop out.

From the rear came an unknown weaver named Henri Renaud, and he was plodding along like the good mill hand he was. He moved from fifty-third place at Framingham to twenty-eighth at Wellesey and finally took the lead two miles from home—and he won in a breeze, finishing four minutes ahead of his closest competitor.

1910

Winner: FRED CAMERON, Nova Scotia. Time: 2h 28m 52s.

One of the true "dark horses" in Marathon history, Fred Cameron, a twenty-three-year-old clerk, stole this race by simply going out in front and staying there all the way. Nobody had ever heard of him and nobody expected such a bold move. Cameron had never run more than ten miles in his life, much less the testing distance of a marathon.

This was also the first Marathon for a runner named Clarence H. DeMar, a man who would create history by winning this race no less than seven times. DeMar finished second but they would hear more of him in the ensuing years. Much more.

Sammy Mellor finished thirty-fourth, by the way.

1911

Winner: CLARENCE H. DEMAR, Melrose, Mass. Time: 2h 21m 39s.

A doctor told Clarence H. DeMar: "Don't run in that race." The physician had found DeMar to have a heart murmur and the thought of him running 24½ miles over country roads and hills and city streets appalled him. So DeMar ran and won—smashing Tom Longboat's record in the bargain.

He ran a supurb race, laying 250 yards off the pace, performing well within himself, before bursting into the lead at Newtonville and riding a slight tail wind into the finish line.

Then Clarence listened to his doctors. He did not compete again until 1917.

1912

Winner: MIKE RYAN, New York City. Time: 2h 21m 18s.

Crash! . . . went Clarence H. DeMar's record, shattered by a full twenty-one seconds by this twenty-three-year-old New Yorker. It wasn't easy. Mike Ryan had to slog through rain and mud but was given a beautiful pace by two runners ahead of him.

First it was Johnny Gallagher, a Yale freshman, who set a blistering pace between the sixth and twenty-first mile. Ryan, remembering how Fred Cameron had "stolen" the race two years earlier, kept close to the collegian. When little Andrew Sockalexis, an Indian lad from Old Town, Maine, took over, Ryan was right after him—and sped past this tired trooper two miles from home.

1913

Winner: FRITZ CARLSON, Minneapolis. Time: 2h 25m 14s.

They say Fritz Carlson didn't "win" this race, but that Andrew Sockalexis, a Penobscot Indian, "lost" it. The Indian ran cautiously through the first half of the contest, remembering the penalty he had paid for his early speed the year before. He was a full five minutes behind the leaders at the halfway mark.

Sockalexis then put on a tremendous burst in the run for home and made a dramatic bid for the lead through the entire length of Beacon Street. But the margin was too great to overcome.

Carlson, a Swedish-born lumberman, was supposed to be too old for this race. He was twenty-nine. He took the lead with four miles to go and came in easily. Sockalexis was second for the second straight year.

1914

Winner: JAMES DUFFY, Hamilton, Ont. Time: 2h 25m 01s.

It was overcast and humid but that didn't stop Jim Duffy, a Sligo-born Ontario longshot, and Edouard Fabre, a sturdy countryman from Montreal, from staging one of the most stirring duels in Marathon history.

The lead changed four times on the run along Beacon Street in Brookline before Duffy pulled away and won by a mere sixty yards—at that time one of the closest margins of all. Fabre was but 14-⅘ths seconds behind at the finish.

1915

Winner: EDOUARD FABRE, Montreal. Time: 2h 31m 41s.

It was a scorching 84 degrees and a third of the field called it quits long before the end. But the sturdy Edouard Fabre, who was so gallant in his loss in 1914, hung in doggedly and wore them all out.

The persistent construction worker was twenty-eight and deemed too old to be taking part in this nonsense of running such long distances. But while others wobbled around him, Fabre took the lead at the railroad bridge at Kenmore Square and achieved the greatest victory of his life.

1916

Winner: ARTHUR ROTH, Roxbury, Mass. Time: 2h 27m 16s.

Now it was truly the "Boston Marathon" as twenty-three-year-old Arthur Roth became the first Boston resident to win the race. It was a popular victory, but mostly a tribute to a canny run put on by Roth, who earned his living as a draftsman.

Again it was a warm day, but Roth went to the front at ten miles and kept pouring it on until he built up a lead of three minutes and seventeen seconds going into the hills. He judged his strength so perfectly that he collapsed as he crossed the finish line and had to be carried to a cot to regain his consciousness.

1917

Winner: BILL KENNEDY, Port Chester, N.Y. Time: 2h 28m 37s.

It was time for the bricklayers of America to rejoice in victory, as courageous Bill Kennedy pulled off one of the most stunning upsets of them all.

He was something else, this thirty-five-year-old gaffer. He caught a freight train to Boston, then slept on a South End pool table the night before the race.

America's entry into World War I was imminent and Kennedy showed up at the starting line giving patriotic speeches. He even stitched an American flag to the knotted handkerchief he was wearing on his head.

But, patriotism aside, Kennedy could run—he beat back the challenge of two favored Finns and even outsped Hannes Kolehmainen, the hero-to-be of the 1920 Olympics. The name of Clarence H. DeMar again appeared in the results, this time as a third-place finisher.

1918

The Marathon was canceled because of World War I; instead, a ten-man military relay race was run over the course to celebrate Patriots' Day. It was won by Camp Devens.

1919

Winner: CARL LINDER, Quincy, Mass. Time: 2h 29m 13s.

The war was over and the runners were back, as beautiful and as bizarre as ever. The winner? He had flat feet. The runner-up? He was just 4-foot-10½.

Carl Linder, who had been New England's decathlon champion, was rejected for military service because of his flat feet. Willie Wick, who was Linder's fellow Quincyite, became the smallest man ever to finish the race.

However, the story of the race revolved around the shoes worn by Chicago's Frank Gillespie. They were brand new and were too tight.

He led from Natick to within 2½ miles of the finish, but his feet were a mass of blisters and blood, even though he had cut off the tops of his shoes during the race, and the pain was just too much for him at the end.

1920

Winner: PETER TRIVOULIDAS, Greece. Time: 2h 29m 31s.

Little Arthur Roth tried to pull off another surprise victory as he had in 1916. He tried again to pace himself to the point of exhaustion at the finish line.

This time his strength gave out at Kenmore Square, and Peter Trivoulidas, a Greek-born busboy living in New York City, came on and won going away.

1921

Winner: FRANK ZUNA, Newark, N.J. Time: 2h 18m 57s.

Make way for the plumbers. Here comes Frank Zuna, showing up at the starting line looking like something less than your ideal hero. He had no bag and he was wearing his running shirt and shoes. His racing shoes were stuffed in his jacket pocket.

Nobody paid much attention to him—until they saw his powerful strides out on the course. He simply ran away from everyone and tore up Mike Ryan's record set in 1912.

Chuck Mellor of Chicago—no relation to our old friend Sammy Mellor—ran stride-for-stride with the winner for seventeen miles. They were friends and it was an amiable duel. Then Zuna took off with the best wishes of his buddy.

1922

Winner: CLARENCE H. DEMAR, Melrose, Mass. Time: 2h 18m 10s.

This was the start of the celebrated "DeMar Era" in the Boston Marathon. This was Clarence H. DeMar's second victory and started a string of five more triumphs in the next eight races—an incredible feat by anyone's standards.

The curious thing is, DeMar did not intend to run in this race, or, for all anyone knew, in any other marathon.

He was back from the war and his printing business was flourishing and he was involved in so many church activities that he just never gave any thought to running again. But during a big sleet storm in November 1921 DeMar found the best means of transportation was by foot. He also found he still enjoyed running.

So he got back into the race and smashed Zuna's record by forty-seven seconds—establishing a permanent mark for the 24½-mile distance.

1923

Winner: CLARENCE H. DEMAR, *Melrose, Mass.* Time: 2h 23m 37s.

This was the last time the race would be run at 24½ miles and Clarence H. DeMar won again. DeMar was back into running on a full-time basis, but his efforts almost led to his demise as a foot racer.

While he was preparing for the 1923 race, he was bitten by a dog as he was running through the snowbanks of Medford. As DeMar was trying to ward off the dog by kicking at him, a man came up behind him and smashed DeMar in the mouth. The blow cut his lip.

"Kick my dog, will you!" the man sneered at DeMar, who offered no retort. His cut developed into erysipelas—an acute disease of the skin —and he was bedded for ten days with his head feeling the size of a pumpkin.

But DeMar recovered in time to win his third Marathon, and he proved he was no fluke by outracing Frank Zuna, the 1921 champion.

(Distance: 26 miles 209 yards)

1924

Winner: CLARENCE H. DEMAR, Melrose, Mass. Time: 2h 29m 40s.

The officials thought they finally had the old Boston course straightened out to measure the required marathon distance of 26 miles 385 yards. It turned out they were a little short.

It didn't matter to Clarence H. DeMar. They probably could have run from Hopkinton to the tip of Cape Cod and he'd have won. In completing his unprecedented three-year sweep, DeMar was at the peak of his running career—at the age of 34.

He simply wiped them all out, running aggressively from start to finish. He took a lead of two hundred yards into the hills and came out of them with a five hundred-yard bulge.

1925

Winner: CHARLES MELLOR, Chicago. Time: 2h 33m.

On one of the coldest days in Marathon history, Charles Mellor ended the three-year reign of the great DeMar. He did it in classic style, too—running in spectacles and gloves, with a wad of tobacco stuffed in his cheek and a morning edition of the *Boston Globe* stuffed inside his shirt to serve as a windbreaker.

DeMar chased Mellor valiantly over the hills, finally coming up to his shoulder at the twenty-three-mile mark. But Mellor, a rugged freight handler, gradually edged away. DeMar had missed his fourth straight by a mere thirty-nine seconds.

1926

Winner: JOHN C. MILES, Nova Scotia. Time: 2h 25m 40s.

This was supposed to be a race between Albin Stenroos, the 1924 Olympic champion from Finland, and Clarence H. DeMar. But the two favorites were upstaged by a nineteen-year-old delivery boy, John C. Miles, who broke the course record in the bargain.

Miles, an apple-cheeked youngster who worked on a grocery wagon, had never run this distance before and nobody gave him much chance.

DeMar was no factor after ten miles. Stenroos was in charge and it seemed like he would stay there, until this young unknown came out of nowhere and began dogging him through the hills.

Miles closed to within ten yards of the pallid Finn's pace, then shot in front when Stenroos came up with a stitch in his side at Boston College.

(Distance: 26 miles 385 yards)

1927

Winner: CLARENCE H. DEMAR, Melrose, Mass. Time: 2h 40m 22s.

They finally got the course squared around so that it was now the official Marathon distance.

And Clarence H. DeMar was on top again, surviving the stifling 82-degree heat to win in almost a walkaway. The remarkable foot racer led at every checkpoint and gained eight hundred yards on the hills alone. Actually, he had it all wrapped up in twenty miles and could have crawled over the hills and still won.

Forty runners dropped out in the first ten miles, such was the heat. DeMar himself lost 5½ pounds. He still won by a smashing 4 minutes 19 seconds.

1928

Winner: CLARENCE H. DEMAR, Melrose, Mass. Time: 2h 37m 7s.

The starting field bulged to 254 runners—a record—but once more it was the old running machine, Clarence H. DeMar, racing away from everyone and even exhausting the supply of adjectives being heaped on him by the sportswriters.

Again DeMar was aggressive from the start. He took charge after the ten-mile mark at Natick and ran solo the rest of the way.

Joey Ray, a celebrated miler of the day, ran in his first Marathon and finished a commendable third. But not before he ran his feet into a mass of blisters and collapsed, utterly spent, at the finish line.

1929

Winner: JOHN C. MILES, Hamilton, Ont. Time: 2h 33m 8s.

The "boy wonder" of the 1926 race returned and won his second laurel wreath. John Miles also smashed Clarence H. DeMar's course record by four minutes.

The youngster, just twenty-two, was haunted by the fact that he had dropped out after only five miles in the 1928 race. He was determined to do something about it and he did.

He waged a tight duel with Whitey Michelson for a full ten miles, from Wellesley to Coolidge Corner. Then the young man broke away and won strongly through the final three miles.

1930

Winner: CLARENCE H. DEMAR, Melrose, Mass. Time: 2h 34m 48s.

This was hail-and-farewell for the old champion, Clarence H. DeMar, the last time he would win the Boston Marathon. Nobody knew it, since the Marathon was now becoming known as: "Isn't that the race DeMar wins every year?"

Anyway, he would run until he was sixty-three years old and turn in a remarkable seventh-place finish at the age of fifty.

Now DeMar simply ran away from two strong Finns, Villar Kyronen and Karl Koski, and might have challenged the course record but for the humid weather, which drained him of his strength.

1931

Winner: JAMES HENIGAN, Medford, Mass. Time: 2h 46m 45s.

This was one of the most popular victories of all time. It came from a man who had tried nine times before and was forced to drop out eight times.

But on his tenth attempt, 38-year-old Jim Henigan, a milkman, the father of four, survived the withering heat and scored his long-awaited victory.

Henigan got a big lift from a tactical blunder by Karl Koski, a Finn. Koski thought Clarence H. DeMar was the man to beat and stayed on his pace.

By the time Koski realized it wasn't going to be DeMar's day—old Clarence ran fifth—it was too late to catch Henigan, who alternately walked and ran the final three miles because of badly blistered feet.

1932

Winner: PAUL DE BRUYN, Germany. Time: 2h 33m 36s.

A blond, beer-drinking, twenty-four-year-old former sailor in the German Navy, Paul de Bruyn came up from his temporary base in New York City to win over Jim Henigan and spoil Henigan's hopes for two in a row.

A Novia Scotia laundryman named John McLeod set a rapid pace and led through the first twenty-one miles. But he went limping off with blistered feet as de Bruyn and Henigan came running by at Cleveland Circle.

The German then won it in the two-mile stretch down Beacon Street.

1933

Winner: LESLIE PAWSON, Pawtucket, R.I. Time: 2h 31m 10s.

A twenty-nine-year-old mill weaver, Leslie Pawson was to score the first of three Marathon victories—and prove a point at the same time.

The old race had been viewed as an endurance contest. Pawson maintained it could be a speed race. So he set out to show them and broke the course record.

It wasn't easy. A strong wind blew straight into the runners, and when Pawson finished a full five minutes ahead of his nearest competitor, his face and arms and legs were windburned to a crisp.

1934

Winner: DAVE KOMONEN, Ontario. Time: 2h 32m 53s.

Again nobody knew it, but this race marked the beginning of a collection of second-place finishes by John Kelley—seven in all (plus two victories).

Dave Komonen, a Finnish-born cobbler living in the Ontario mining country, made his own shoes and ran away with the race. It almost seemed like he was on roller skates. He beat Kelley by almost four minutes.

1935

Winner: JOHN A. KELLEY, Arlington, Mass. Time: 2h 32m 7s.

For all his legendary breakdowns in the closing stages, John Kelley won this race rather easily. When he got sick, near the end, he merely stuck his finger down his throat and regurgitated his troubles away.

It was not to be so easy for him in the future.

Kelley hooked up in an early duel with Dave Komonen, who had beaten him the year before, But the Finn soon retired from the race. He took a car back to Boston and was so sure of Kelley's victory that he scribbled him a note of congratulations and left it at the Lenox Hotel before starting back home to Canada.

1936

Winner: ELLISON M. (TARZAN) BROWN, Alton, R.I. Time: 2h 33m 40s.

This was one of the wildest of all Marathons, with Tarzan Brown, a Narragansett Indian, running ahead of everyone at the outset—including the press cars. He beat the writers—and everyone else—into Framingham, the first checkpoint, and was five hundred yards ahead.

Brown opened his lead to nine hundred yards—nine football fields—going into the hills of Newton. Here, Johnny Kelley put on one of the greatest runs ever staged through the hills and caught up to Brown.

But Kelley made the mistake of patting the Indian on the backside as he was about to pass him, and that awoke Brown. He was off to

178

the races again, taking another lead, which enabled him to all but walk home. Kelley, spent, began to stagger and finished fifth.

1937

Winner: WALTER YOUNG, Quebec. Time: 2h 33m 20s.

Now it was a snowshoe racer who won the Marathon. It was Walter Young, an unemployed Canadian, who raced in both the winter and summer.

Now wearing running shoes, he engaged in a tremendous duel with John Kelley. They battled for a full twenty-three miles, with the lead changing sixteen times.

Kelley made his big move at twenty miles, pulling ahead to a hundred-yard lead. But Young, who was an amateur boxer, caught him and his superior strength prevailed, until he beat "Kel" by almost six minutes.

1938

Winner: LESLIE PAWSON, Pawtucket, R.I. Time: 2h 35m 34s.

Five years after winning his first Marathon—and his record still stood—Leslie Pawson came back to become the fourth repeater in Boston.

It was a hot day, with the temperature hitting 75 degrees, and it became a race of attrition.

Duncan McCallum from Canada led the way for eight miles, when John Kelley took over from the eighth through the fifteenth mile. Pawson stayed right after him and again Kelley couldn't sustain the pace.

Pawson was weary at the end but his big effort over the hills was enough to sustain him to the finish line. Pat Dengis was second and Kelley third.

1939

Winner: ELLISON M. (TARZAN) BROWN, Alton, R.I. Time: 2h 28m 52s.

The Indian was back—and this time with a record run. A little wiser and more mature, Tarzan Brown paced himself for a change and brought down Leslie Pawson's record on a cold, drizzly day.

Tarzan let the others go out front this time. He moved up with the leaders at the eight-mile mark and fought, almost shoulder to shoulder, with Walter Young, a gangling Canadian, through the seventeen-mile mark.

But Brown was running beautifully—fluidly—and with his tan body glistening in the rain, he pulled ahead and romped home an easy winner. He now held every checkpoint record on the course—from Framingham to the tape.

1940

Winner: GERARD COTE, Quebec. Time: 2h 28m 28s.

A notable race—for there went Tarzan Brown's record after only one year and this marked the start of the "Cote Era." The freewheeling Frenchman would win four Marathons, a mark second only to Clarence H. DeMar's seven titles—and he would win them in grand fashion.

This time Gerard Cote would take them all by surprise. Nobody knew anything about him, so nobody paid much attention to him.

He came out of fifth place, knocked off Brown and Leslie Pawson, then set his sights on the leader—John Kelley. He disposed of "Kel" at the twenty-mile mark and, with an odd flip-flopping style—as if he were wearing snowshoes—he cruised in with his record-smashing performance.

Cote then lit up his victory cigar—long before anyone in Boston ever heard of Red Auerbach.

1941

Winner: LESLIE PAWSON, Pawtucket, R.I. Time: 2h 30m 38s.

Now thirty-seven years old, Leslie Pawson won his third—and final—Marathon with a powerful run on a hot day.

It was 72 degrees and Pawson ran his familiar race. He broke strongly, then made his bid in the middle of the race. He was trailing five men—among them former champions Gerard Cote, John Kelley and Tarzan Brown—when he went into high gear.

Only Kelley attempted to stay with him. They fought for eight miles, into and over the hills, before Pawson slowly edged ahead.

Poor "Kel"—he was on Exeter Street, only 220 yards behind, when he saw Pawson finish. It was just one of many frustrations for the popular Irishman.

1942

Winner: BERNARD JOSEPH SMITH, Medford, Mass. Time: 2h 26m 51s.

World War II was raging and most people had their minds on other things. And so it was a tremendous surprise when this lanky milkman came on and not only won the Marathon but smashed Gerard Cote's record.

Joe Smith, an A.A.U. distance champion, wasn't even going to run. He was sick on the morning of the race. He was finally talked into it by his wife—and this was to be the first profound effect women would have on the old race. We would hear more from them later on.

It was an icy day—with the temperature down to 44 degrees—and Smith ran a beautiful race. Swirling along with long strides, he swept into the lead when they came out of the hills and nobody ever saw him again.

1943

Winner: GERARD COTE, Quebec. Time: 2h 28m 25s.

Gerard Cote was now a commando in the Canadian Army, but they gave him time off to run in the Marathon. He made the most of the chance by winning his second championship.

And he ran despite a strained Achilles' tendon, a mishap from training camp.

Cote, who liked the good life—a smoke, a drink and dancing— brought his wife with him and she saw her husband engage in a hot duel with John Kelley.

They staged a furious battle over twenty-one miles with Cote finally pulling away in the closing stages.

1944

Winner: GERARD COTE, Quebec. Time: 2h 31m 50s.

The script was the same as the year before—Gerard Cote first and John Kelley second—and this one was closer than ever. Cote won by only sixty yards, a mere thirteen seconds over the dogged but frustrated Irishman.

The two of them engaged in a long and persistent chase over the hills. Kelley threw no fewer than seven sprints at Cote. The Canadian soldier withstood them all.

They were still running together with seven hundred yards to go before Cote edged ahead. All Kelley could do now was shake his head in despair. He would finish second for the sixth time.

1945

Winner: JOHN A. KELLEY, Arlington, Mass. Time: 2h 30m 40s.

A soldier boy now, John Kelley's "great faith" was finally rewarded with his second win in the Marathon. And it was a beauty. He didn't falter a single step of the way—not even over those final miles that had proved so fatal to him in the past.

If anything, Kelley ran like a "buzz bomb" through the final stages as he careened to victory.

Nothing bothered him on this day, and at thirty-seven, Kelley smiled at the finish and said: "Life begins at 40—and I have three more years to go!"

It was to be his last victory, however—though he would run and run for decades to come.

1946

Winner: STYLIANOS KYRIAKIDES, Greece. Time: 2h 29m 27s.

Jerry Nason calls this the "most significant B.A.A. race of all time." It was won by the almost fanatical determination of the gaunt Greek, Stylianos Kyriakides, who was running to dramatize the plight of his starving countrymen.

It also marked the start of a great foreign onslaught on the Marathon.

Kyriakides, himself a victim of malnutrition, caught Johnny Kelley with only 1½ miles to go and gutted it out to the finish line. His sensational feat—which received world acclaim—triggered a flood of foreign aid to Greece.

This race also marked the last time press cars were allowed on the course. From now on, gents, you take the bus.

1947

Winner: YUN BOK SUH, Korea. Time: 2h 25m 39s.

Now it was the Orientals' turn to make their first mark on the Marathon as Yun Bok Suh, at 5-foot-1 the smallest man ever to win the race, swept home in front despite all sorts of difficulties.

He was knocked down by a a fox terrier bounding onto the course and suffered a cut knee. His shoelaces broke. But the little guy—sent here through contributions of American G.I.'s in Korea—still ran at a record pace. In fact, he was flying like a windblown leaf at the finish line as he broke Joe Smith's record of 1942.

1948

Winner: GERARD COTE, Quebec. Time: 2h 31m 2s.

The jovial Canadian Gerard Cote was back to prove that his victories in 1943 and 1944 were no wartime flukes. This was his fourth Marathon triumph, second only to Clarence H. DeMar's record of seven, and it was a hard-fought victory.

Cote exchanged insults in an elbow-to-elbow duel with Ted Vogel of Watertown, Massachusetts. They battled for twenty-three miles and nearly came to blows.

Vogel became incensed when Cote kept crisscrossing in front of him. He felt the tactics were unethical. Cote kept right on going, however, and both cooled down after the race.

1949

Winner: KARL GOSTA LEANDERSSON, Sweden. Time: 2h 31m 50s.

The tall, blond, blue-eyed Swede wanted to make sure he was ready for his Boston test, so he ran the course ten days before the race—and broke the record.

He also injured his Achilles' tendon.

Luckily, the tendon mended in time and Karl Gosta Leandersson won easily—except for that woman driver who zipped out of a side road in Auburndale and almost struck him.

1950

Winner: KEE YONG HAM, Korea. Time: 2h 32m 39s.

Ham—quickly dubbed "Swift Premium" by the writers—led a 1-2-3 sweep by the Koreans.

Kee Yong Ham was rated no better than the No. 3 man on his team, but even though he walked four different times in the final four miles, he built up such a large margin that he finished 3 minutes 19 seconds before Kil Yoon Song. Yun Chil Choi, the Korean national champion, was third.

1951

Winner: SHIGEKI TANAKA, Japan. Time: 2h 27m 45s.

This nineteen-year-old student became one of the youngest winners in Boston with an exciting run over the hills of Newton. And his victory had a historic note to it. Shigeki Tanaka was born in Hiroshima, where America's first atom bomb fell in World War II.

Tanaka was rated no better than his country's fourth-best runner, but he left them all gasping when he came down from the hills.

1952

Winner: DOROTEO FLORES, Guatemala. Time: 2h 31m 53s.

It was a blazing 88 degrees—sheer murder for most of the field—but an ideal day for this swarthy Indian. Doroteo Flores had a poor-paying job in a Guatemala mill, so what was a little more heat?

While others fell all around him, Flores ran away and won by almost five minutes. Oddly enough, the hatchet-faced Central American had never run 26 miles 385 yards before. It was a good thing nobody told him how tough it was.

1953

Winner: KEIZO YAMADA, Japan. Time: 2h 18m 51s.

Because of construction along the route, the course accidently dropped in length to 25 miles 938 yards. The error wasn't discovered until times in ensuing races began sounding suspicious.

This may—or may not—have accounted for Keizo Yamada's record-breaking time. No one will ever be able to tell.

In any event the 108-pounder was the best out there and won by surviving a tough three-way struggle, finishing just twenty-eight seconds ahead of Finland's Veikko Karvonen and forty-five seconds ahead of Sweden's Karl Gosta Leandersson. The Americans were nowhere to be found—a circumstance that was now expected in these postwar races. The foreigners seemed to have more time—and support—for their training.

1954

Winner: VEIKKO KARVONEN, Finland. Time: 2h 20m 39s.

This race produced an "all-star" field, composed of Jim Peters, England's world record-holder; Delfo Cabera of Argentina, the 1948 Olympic champion; Karau Hiroshima, a Japanese champion; Erkki Puolakka, a Finnish titlist, and John J. (The Younger) Kelley, the American A.A.U. champion.

Veikko Karvonen, a chunky postal clerk, outran them all.

Peters set the pace from the eighth to the eighteenth mile, with Karvonen hounding him every step of the way. When leg cramps clutched at Peters in West Newton, Karvonen took over and won by two minutes.

1955

Winner: HIDEO HAMAMURA, Japan. Time: 2h 18m 22s.

Again the record fell—this time on a great second-half run by Hideo Hamamura. He was in tenth position when he made his move.

Hamamura took the lead along Beacon Street, 3¼ miles from the finish, and clipped countryman Keizo Yamada's record by twenty-nine seconds.

Hamamura's strength in the hills dismayed all those around him.

1956

Winner: ANTTI VISKARI, Finland. Time: 2h 14m 14s.

The course obviously had to be checked after this race. The times were too fast.

Again the record was broken as Sgt. Antti Viskari, a Finnish soldier, hooked up in a tremendous duel with John (The Younger) Kelley.

Viskari pulled away in the final mile and beat Kelley by nineteen seconds.

1957

Winner: JOHN J. KELLEY, Groton, Conn. Time: 2h 20m 05s.

With the course now accurately measured, John (The Younger) Kelley gave America its first postwar victory and broke a string of eleven foreign wins.

He also broke the course record—and his mark became the accepted mark.

Kelley was never threatened as he disposed of three Japanese, two Finns, three Koreans, a Mexican, several Canadians and a host of Americans.

Walter A. Brown was so pleased to have an American winner again that he gave Kelley a gold watch after the race, suitably inscribed.

1958

Winner: FRANJO MIHALIC, Yugoslavia. Time: 2h 25m 54s.

Oops, there goes America's brief hold on the Marathon. The foreign contingent was back as Franjo Mihalic—the Olympic runner-up in 1956—ran well over the sunbaked course. It was 84 degrees but it didn't seem to bother the Yugoslav printer.

All Mihalic did was filch a table napkin from the Lenox Hotel and stitch it to his sun visor to protect his balding head—and away he went.

Johnny (The Younger)—no relation to Johnny The Elder—Kelley finished second, and the runner-up spot would haunt him as it had Johnny (The Elder) Kelley. The Younger would finish second five times in his Boston career.

1959

Winner: EINO OKSANEN, Finland. Time: 2h 22m 42s.

A 154-pound Helsinki police detective, Eino Oksanen beat back John (The Younger) Kelley to win the first of his three Boston Marathon titles.

In fact, Oksanen was to become known as The Ox for his bullish strength in the stretch. This time he withstood no less than nine "sprints" by Kelley to win the race.

The conditions were atrocious—42 degrees with a cold head wind blowing into the runners' faces and rain pelting them soon after leaving Hopkinton. But Oksanen weathered all the storms to win by a minute and a second over Kelley.

1960

Winner: PAAVO KOTILA, Finland. Time: 2h 20m 54s.

The 1959 winner, Eino Oksanen, stayed home and it may have been a blunder on his part. It may have cost him a chance to win an unprecedented four straight Boston Marathons.

As it was, a countryman made a shambles of the U.S. Olympic trial by simply setting a dazzling pace in the middle of the race.

All that made it close is that Paavo Kotila had no opposition. Gordon McKenzie of New York came on at the end to make it fairly close but was still some ninety seconds behind at the finish.

For the first time, John (The Younger) Kelley failed to finish.

1961

Winner: EINO OKSANEN, Finland. Time: 2h 23m 39s.

It could be said that a black dog decided the 1961 Boston Marathon as John (The Younger) Kelley, running shoulder to shoulder with Eino Oksanen and Jim Norris, was sent sprawling by the pooch at the sixteen-mile mark.

Kelley went down hard, suffering cuts on his elbow and knee. In an unprecented show of sportsmanship, Norris went back and hauled Kelley to his legs and got him running again.

Showing great determination, Kelley caught up to Oksanen—and even took a slight lead into the hills of Newton—but his stamina had been taxed, his rhythm upset and he fell behind at the end, losing by a mere twenty-five seconds. At a biting 39 degrees, this was the coldest race since 1925.

1962

Winner: EINO OKSANEN, Finland. Time: 2h 23m 48s.

Eino Oksanen, the indomitable Ox, won his third Boston Marathon and it was the easiest of all. He kept looking back for his familiar pursuer, John (The Younger) Kelley, but this wasn't to be Kelley's day. He finished in fourth place, almost five minutes off the winner's pace.

Oksanen beat back his first challenger, U.S. Marine Lt. Alex Breckenridge, at the sixteen-mile mark, then disposed of compatriot Paavo Pystnen at the 20½-mile mark.

Kelley, ever the sportsman, called Oksanen's three victories (in three straight tries, really) as good as Clarence H. DeMar's seven triumphs since Oksanen was up against faster runners.

1963

Winner: AURELE VANDENDRIESSCHE, Belgium. Time: 2h 18m 58s.

This race was supposed to be a showcase for the world's fastest marathon runner, Ethiopia's Abebe Bikila, who was in the midst of winning two straight Olympic gold medals (1960 and 1964).

And for eighteen miles it looked just that way—a runaway for Bikila, who was being spurred on by countryman, Mamo Wolde (who would win an Olympic gold medal for himself in 1968).

But then the cold chill of New England and the tough, old course began getting to the two Ethiopians. Bikila was struck by leg cramps (he would finish fifth) and Wolde just slowed down (he finished ninth).

Out of nowhere came Aurele Vandendriessche (pronounced vanDEN-dreeYESH) to race home in front in record-breaking time. Johnny (The Younger) Kelley was back in his familiar role of runner-up, finishing second for the fifth time in his career.

1964

Winner: AURELE VANDENDRIESSCHE, Belgium. Time: 2h 19m 59s.

It was another cold day, this time with a wet snow pelting the runners. The field went over 300 for the first time, with 301 trying the old course.

Aurele Vandendriessche won his second straight title by mounting a savage attack over the hills. Everyone literally crumbled at his heels.

Hal Higdon, the author-runner, was the top American finisher.

1965

Winner: MORIO SHIGEMATSU, Japan. Time: 2h 16m 33s.

This would start an extraordinary two-year dominance by Japan. The unknown Morio Shigematsu, rated no better than No. 4 among five Japanese entries, led a 1-2-3-5-6 Nippon sweep.

Only defender Aurele Vandendriessche's fourth-place spot broke up the Japanese monopoly.

The finish of the race was moved from the old Lenox Hotel to the Prudential Center. To keep the distance intact, race director Will Cloney moved the starting line back 389 yards in Hopkinton.

They could have run up the side of Fujiyama and Shigematsu probably could have beaten them all. He simply sustained his speed over the entire distance and shattered the course record.

1966

Winner: KENJI KIMIHARA, Japan. Time: 2h 17m 11s.

The Japanese won even more convincingly than in 1965, sweeping the top four places this time. And again it was not Japan's top man who took the honors.

The race was supposed to be won by Toru Terasawa, the Japanese champion. But little Kenji Kimihara, no better than the No. 3 man, made a mad rush from his fourth position to win in the last two miles.

He not only had to battle three of his countrymen but had to overcome a stiff eighteen-mile-an-hour head wind.

A woman, Roberta Gibb, ran unofficially and went the full distance.

1967

Winner: DAVID McKENZIE, New Zealand. Time: 2h 15m 45s.

Now there was a real mob scene out in Hopkinton—601 starters—and they staged the fastest mass race in the history of the Boston Marathon. A total of 479 competitors finished with David McKenzie setting a course record.

The New Zealand printer exploded on the rain-slick hills of Newton to leave behind all of his challengers. Tom Laris, a Dartmouth alumnus from California, put on a game bid at the end and finished second.

The race was marred by a shoving incident as Jock Semple tried to tear the number from a woman competitor, K. Switzer.

1968

Winner: AMBROSE BURFOOT, Groton, Conn. Time: 2h 22m 17s.

Amby Burfoot, a reed-like runner from Wesleyan University, gave America its first victory in ten years as the field swelled to more than 900 runners.

Burfoot was coached by the last American winner, Johnny (The Younger) Kelley. The 6-foot-140-pound Burfoot learned his lessons well as he sprinted away to a thirty-eight-second victory in the last five miles.

Curiously, three of the top runners—Agustin Calle of Colombia, Pat McMahon of Ireland and Tom Laris of the United States—withdrew the day before the race.

The Boston Marathon

1969

Winner: YOSHIAKI UNETANI, Japan. Time: 2h 13m 49s.

Now the field topped the 1,000 mark with 1,150 starters, the last of the "open" races in Boston. Henceforth, there would be qualifying times set by the officials.

This was a perfect day for running—55 degrees and no wind whatever—and Yoshiaki Unetani broke the course record by almost two minutes.

Unetani might have even gone faster except he had no competition at all over the final nine miles.

1970

Winner: RON HILL, England. Time: 2h 10m 30s.

Now the runners had to qualify by running a marathon in less than four hours (or its equivalent at shorter distances). The harried officials of the race imposed this rule to cut down on the unwieldy field.

It didn't do much good. A total of 1,011 starters still went romping through the countryside—but none faster than Ron Hill.

It was another wet day—rain and 44 degrees—but it was good for running and not only did Hill break the course record, but Eamon O'Reilly from Washington, D.C., set an American record and finished second.

1971

Winner: ALVARO MEJIA, Colombia. Time: 2h 18m 45s.

Still dismayed at the size of the field, officials now dropped the qualifying time to 3:30—and the field fell below the 1,000 mark, down to 887 starters.

This turned out to be the closest race in the history of the Boston Marathon. Alvaro Mejia and Irishman Pat McMahon virtually ran shoulder to shoulder right into the Prudential Center before Mejia pulled away to a five-second victory.

1972

Winner: OLAVI SUOMALAINEN, Finland. Time: 2h 15m 39s.

Welcome aboard, ladies! The women were permitted to run officially for the fist time and Nina Kuscsik became their first champion at 3:10.26.

As for the men, the winner was a Finnish strider filled with vowels, consonants, long hair and a big smile.

Olavi Suomalainen, ranked only fourth in his country, won by pulling away from Mexico's Victor Mora at Lake Street in Chestnut Hill.

1973

Winner: JON ANDERSON, Eugene, Ore. Time: 2h 16m 03s.

Americans were back on top as Jon Anderson, a conscientious objector who was doing his service time as a dishwasher, raced home in front of New Jersey's Tom Fleming.

Anderson took command at the twenty-mile mark and was never headed as he gave the United States its first victory in five years.

Anderson, twenty-three, was working in a California hospital in lieu of military duty, getting up at 5:30 to do his training before reporting to work. His victory, coming after Frank Shorter's Olympic triumph in Munich the year before, put the United States in the forefront of marathon running.

The women's winner was Jacqueline Hansen of Granda Hills, California. She finished in 3h 06m 26s.

1974

Winner: NEIL CUSACK, Ireland. Time: 2h 13m 39s.

Neil Cusack, an Irishman by way of Johnson City, Tenn., took on the speediest runners and ran away to victory in a display of style and stamina.

Just twenty-two and wearing a Robin Hood beard, Cusack ran without a number on his chest. It fluttered to the roadside as he roared through Wellesley College to the shrieks of coeds.

Cusack won by forty-six seconds over Tom Fleming, who was runner-up for the second year in a row. The ladies were led by Mrs. Gorman, thirty-eight, of Los Angeles, a fleet flyer of only 89 pounds.

1975

Winner: WILL RODGERS, Boston. Time: 2h 09m 55s.

The twenty-seven-year-old Boston College student Will Rodgers stopped five times along the way—four times for water and once to tie his shoelace—and still ran faster than anyone in the history of the Boston Marathon.

The race drew an almost unbelievable field of 2,041 starters and they were piling up in such staggering numbers that the line was two city blocks in length.

Leading the way for the ladies was Liane Winter of West Germany. Her time was 2h 42m 24s, a world record. Rodgers couldn't believe his own time. "It just freaks me out to think I went that fast," he said.

1976

Winner: JACK FULTZ, Franklin, Pa. Time: 2h 20m 19s.

It was a scorching day—91 degrees in the shade and 116 in the sun. The runners literally ran through a rainbow of garden hoses from Hopkinton to Boston.

In fact, they called this race the "Run for the Hoses." It was the hottest marathon in history and more than 40 percent of the 1,898 starters failed to finish.

Jack Fultz, a Georgetown student, won this race of attrition despite a cramp in his leg. A pigtailed blonde named Kim Merritt, twenty, from Wisconsin, lead the women in 2h 47m 10s—and was immediately taken to the hospital suffering from exhaustion.

Index

Index

A

Ahern, John, 44
Amateur Athletic Union (A.A.U.), 96, 109–10
Anderson, Jon, 165, 191
Answell, Gideon, 97
Ashland (Massachusetts), 21
   Metcalfe's Mill, 8
Associated Press bureau (Richmond), 102
Athens (Greece), 31
   Olympic Marathon in (1896), 7, 13, 31
Auerbach, Red, 94, 115

B

B.A.A., *see* Boston Athletic Association

Barry, Bill, 19
Barry, Jack, 45
Bath (Maine), marathon in, 71
Beacon Street (Boston), 21
Beef stew, vi, 18, 115
Belle Isle (Detroit), 130
Berlin, Olympic Marathon in (1936), 41, 74–77
Berman, Alan, 160
Bikila, Abebe, 34, 187–88
Black runners, 123
Blind runners, 135–40
Bocci, Jeanne, 55, 129–32
Bocci, Jerry, 55, 130–34
Boston (Massachusetts)
   Beacon Street, 21
   Chestnut Hill Avenue, 21
   Cleveland Circle, 21
   Commonwealth Avenue, 21
   Hereford Street, 21
   Irvington Street Oval, 8

Kenmore Square, 21
Massachusetts Avenue, 165
Prudential Building, 16, 18, 21,
  23, 93, 153, 188
Boston Athletic Assocciation
  (B.A.A.), 7, 8, 85, 90, 93
Boston Globe, 9, 10, 132
Boston Marathon
  beef stew for, vi, 18, 115
  black runners in, 123
  blind runners in, 135–40
  champions, 163–192
  distance of, 23, 165, 174, 175,
    184, 188
  dog menace in, 149–51, 183, 187
  history of, 13, 23
  international competitors in,
    119–20
  last-place finishes in, 158–62
  married couples in, 55, 130–32
  medical aid at, 152–56
  Olympic Marathon runners in,
    33–34
  prizes in, 119
  qualifying times required for,
    190
  record time (1975), 24, 113,
    191–92
  route of, 21
  wheelchair competitors in, 146–
    48
  women in, *see* Women runners
  women's world record in (1975),
    192
Bourdelais, Clovis, 15
Breckenridge, Alex, 187
Brederson, Jake, 161
Briggs, Arnie, 96, 103–8
  in shoving incident with Semple,
    108

Switzer and, 103–6
Brignolia, Lawrence, 163, 166
Brown, Ellison Myers (Tarzan),
  40–45, 77, 125
  as champion (1936), 41, 164,
    178–79
  as champion (1939), 164, 179–
    80
  defeats J. A. Kelley (1936), 40–
    41, 178–79
  on DeMar, 45
  disqualified from Berlin Olympic
    Marathon (1936), 41
  home on Narragansett Indian
    reservation, 40–43
  killed in car accident (1975),
    45
Brown, Ethel Wilcox, 43
Brown, George, Jr., 13, 15
Brown, George V., Sr., 13
Brown, Tom, 11, 13
Brown, Walter A., 13, 39, 151, 186
Bruyn, Paul de, 164, 177
Burfoot, Ambrose, 89, 165, 189
Burke, Tom, 8

C

Cabera, Delfo, 33, 185
Caffrey, James J., 163, 166, 167
Calle, Agustin, 189
Cameron, Fred, 163, 169, 170
Carlson, Fritz, 163
Cataldo, Tony, 19–20
Cavanaugh, Marty, 76
Cerutty, Percy, 22
Chestnut Hill Avenue (Boston), 21
Chodes, John, 126–27
Cleveland Circle (Boston), 21

Cloney, Will, 117–21, 188
 Switzer and, 107
 women given permission to com-
  pete by, 93
Cobb, Marguerite F., 156
Collins, Bud, 95
Collins, George, 118
Commonwealth Avenue (Boston),
 21
Concannon, Joe, 24
Confalone, Al, 128
Connolly, Thomas, 152–55
Connors, Jimmy (Cigars), 7
Constantine (prince of Greece), 32
Cope, Myron, 113
Corbitt, Ted, 122–28
Cote, Gerald, 80–86
 as champion, 164, 180–83
 charged with unfair tactics by
  Vogel, 85, 183
 defeats J. A. Kelley (1940, 1943,
  1944), 82, 84–85, 180–83
 Gavuzzi and, 81, 83
 Seaver and, 83
Coyle, Gerald, 46–47, 51–66
Coyle, Pat, 54, 56–57
Crane, Tom, 85
Cunningham, Glenn, 45
Cusack, Neil, 165, 191

D

Daley, Arthur, 87
Davis, Bill, 166
DeMar, Clarence H., 67–73, 150,
 172, 177
 Tarzan Brown on, 45
 as champion, 163–64, 170, 173–
  77

Egan on, 67–68
 injured (1923), 174
 J. A. Kelley on, 78
 Nason on, 36
 in second place, 169–70, 175
 Timpany on, 161–62
 warned of heart problem, 68–69,
  154, 170
Dengis, Pat, 120, 150
Detroit (Michigan)
 Belle Isle, 130
 Windmill Point, 132
Devens, Camp, 172
Dog Control Service, 151
Dog menace, 149–51, 174, 183,
 187
Duffy, James, 163, 171

E

Edwards, Phillip, 45
Egan, David, 38, 67–68
Exeter Street (Hopkinton), 23

F

Fabre, Edouard, 163, 171
First Congregational Church (Hop-
 kinton), 93
Fish, Howard MacFarland, Jr., 96
Fish, Marjorie, 96
Fitzgerald, Ray, 1, 145, 146
Fleming, Tom, 90, 191
Flores, Doroteo, 164
Flynn, Dick, 20
Foley, Peter, 6, 76
Ford, Timothy, 163, 168

Framingham (Massachusetts), 21
Fultz, Jack, 165, 192

G

Gallagher, Johnny, 170
Gantz, Walt, 16–17
Gavuzzi, Pete, 81, 83
George (prince of Greece), 32
Gibb, Roberta Louise, 92–93, 96
    as first woman runner (1966),
        92–93, 104, 189
    reactions to, 93–95
Gillespie, Frank, 172–73
Glickman, Marty, 77
Gorman, Mrs., 191
Gray, Hamilton, 165–66
Great Britain, marathon in (1973),
    123
Gregory, Lou, 120
Grieve, Bob, 103

H

Hall, Bob, 146–47
Hamamura, Hideo, 164, 185
Hamilton, Scott Downs, Jr., 15
Hansen, Jaqueline, 97, 191
Hayden Rowe (Hopkinton), 21
Hayes, John, 33, 169
Heartbreak Hill, 22, 29, 64
Helsinki, Olympic Marathon in
    (1952), 124
Henigan, James, 164, 177
Hereford Street (Boston), 21
Hicks, Tom, 33, 168
Higdon, Hal, 159, 188
Hill, Ron, 165, 190

Hiroshima, Karau, 185
Honeywell Corporation, 18, 121
Hopkinton (Massachusetts), 11–
    12, 14, 51–52, 120, 188
    Exeter Street, 23
    First Congregational Church in,
        93
    Hayden Rowe and Town Green,
        21
    Lenox Hotel in, 23, 188
    Marathon Inn, 14
    Walter A. Brown School, 13
Hughson, Frank, 166
Hunter, James (Catfish), 1

I

International champions, 39, 40,
    182–85
    See also specific champions
Irvington Street Oval (Boston), 8
Israel, Richard J., 3–5
Issacs, Stan, 47

J

Japanese Athletic Association, 90
Jokl, Ernest, 156

K

Karvonen, Veikko, 164, 184, 185
Katzew, Amy, 156
Keane, Clif, 115
Kee Yong Ham, 164, 183–84
Keiss, Bob, 23, 46–51, 60, 63

Kelley, John A., 53, 74–79, 104, 179
  at Berlin Olympic Marathon (1936), 75–77
  Tarzan Brown and, 40–41, 45, 178–79
  as champion (1935), 75, 164, 178
  as champion (1945), 75, 78–79, 85, 182
  defeated by Cote (1940, 1943, 1944), 82, 84–85, 180–83
  defeated by Kyriakides (1946), 39
  on DeMar, 78
  at London Olympic Marathon (1948), 76, 77
  on Owens, 77
  in second place, 75, 178–83
Kelley, John J., 185, 187
  as champion (1957), 164, 185–86
  as coach for Burfoot, 189
  knocked down by dog (1961), 150, 151, 187
  in second place, 185–88
Kelly, John, 78
Kenmore Square (Boston), 21
Kennedy, Bill, 164, 172
Kil Yoon Song, 184
Kimihara, Kenji, 165, 189
Kindlan, Hugh, vi
Kneeland, Dave, 168
Koch, Ellery, 15
Koen, Fanny Blankers, 95
Kolehmainen, Hans, 33, 172
Komonen, Dave, 37, 164, 178
Koski, Karl, 177
Kotila, Paavo, 165, 186–87
Kraft, Alexa, 55, 129–32

Kraft, Martin, 55, 129–33
Kryonen, Villar, 176
Kuscsik, Nina, 17, 96, 190
Kyriakides, Stylianos, 39, 164, 182

L

Lafferty, Johnny, 128
LaGuardia, Fiorello, 104
Laris, Tom, 189
Last-place finishes, 158–62
Leandersson, Karl Gosta, 164, 183, 184
Lee, James, 168
Lee, Leo, 160, 161
Lenox Hotel (Hopkinton), 23, 188
Leonard, Tommy, 23–30
Linden, Don, 19
Linder, Carl, 164, 172
Linscott, John, 110–11
Lombardi, Vince, 87–88
London
  1908 Olympic Marathon in, 23, 33
  1948 Olympic Marathon in, 77, 95
Longboat, Tom, 64, 163, 168–69
Lorden, John C., 163, 167
Lorz, Fred, 33, 163, 168
Love Story (Love and Death) (Segal), 141, 143
Loues, Spiridon, 7, 32

M

McCallum, Duncan, 179
McCurdy, Bill, 143

McDermott, John J., 7, 9, 163, 165
McDonald, Ronald J., 163, 165–67
McDonough, Will, 146
McKenzie, David, 165, 189
McLeod, John, 177
McMahon, Pat, 89, 189, 190
McMannus, Frances, 12
Manchester (New Hampshire), 41
Mantle, Mickey, 87, 88
Marathon (Greece), 31, 32
Marathon
  in Bath (Maine), 71
  in Great Britain, 123
  in Manchester (New Hampshire), 41
  from New York City to LaGuardia Airport, 104
  in Philadelphia, 78
  from Stamford (Connecticut) to New York City, 7, 165
  Wheelchair, 147
  See also Boston Marathon; Olympic Marathon
Marathon Inn (Hopkinton), 14
Married couples, 55, 130–32
Massachusetts Avenue (Boston), 165
Massachusetts Society for the Prevention of Cruelty to Animals, 151
Maule, Tex, 86
Medical aid, 16, 18–20, 152–56
Mejia, Alvaro, 89, 165, 190
Mellor, Charles, 7, 164, 173
Mellor, Sammy, 163, 167, 168, 170
Merritt, Kim, 192
Metcalfe's Mill (Ashland), 8
Michelson, Whitey, 176
Mihalic, Franjo, 164, 186
Miles, John C., 164, 175, 176

Miller, Tom, 96, 106, 108–9
  in shoving incident with Semple, 108
Moloney, Frank, 118
Montville, Leight, 137
Moody, Charlie, 167
Mora, Victor, 191
Morrissey, Thomas, 163, 169
Mungoven, John F., 140
Munich, Olympic Marathon in (1972), 33

N

Nason, Jerry, 35–44, 80, 107
  on Tarzan Brown, 40–44
  on DeMar, 35
  on women runners, 95
Natick (Massachusetts), 21
Newton Hills, 21, 22, 61
Newton Lower Falls, 21
New York City marathon
  to LaGuardia Airport, 104
  from Stamford (Connecticut) to, 7, 165
Norris, Jim, 151, 187
North Medford Club, 161

O

O'Connor, Neil, 55
Oksanen, Eino, 151, 164, 165, 186, 187
Olympic Marathon
  1896 (Athens), 7, 13, 31
  1903 (St. Louis), 33, 168

1908 (London), 23, 33
1936 (Berlin), 41, 74–77
1948 (London), 76, 77, 95
1952 (Helsinki), 124
1972 (Munich), 33
history of, 7, 31–33
Olympic marathoners in Boston
Marathon, 33–34
O'Reilly, Eamon, 190
Osler, Tom, 150
Owens, Jesse, 77

P

Palmer, Arthur, 72
Pape, Robert, 15
Pardo, Joe, 52–53, 135–37
Pawson, Leslie, 85, 164, 177–80
Peters, Jim, 185
Pheidippides, 7, 31
Philadelphia Marathon, 78
Pietri, Dorando, 33
Power, Larry, 49, 55
Prizes, 119
Prudential Building (Prudential
Center Plaza), 16, 21, 93, 153
finishing line moved to (1965),
18, 23, 188
Prudential Insurance Company,
18–20, 117–18, 155
Puolakka, Erkki, 185
Pystnen, Paavo, 187

Q

Qualifying times, 190

R

Rankin, Scott, 84
Ray, Joey, 176
Record times (1975), 24, 113,
191–92
Renaud, Henri, 163, 169
Revere, Paul, 8
Roberts, Gene, 146–48
Rodgers, Will, 24, 27, 88–91
as champion (1975), 3, 165,
191–92
record time of, 113, 191–92
stops during Marathon (1975),
88–89, 191–92
Roth, Arthur, 164, 171–73
Route of Boston Marathon, 21
Runners' World, The (Osler), 150
Ruthrauff, William, 127
Ryan, Mike, 163, 170

S

Sabbag, Bob, 19
St. Louis Olympic Marathon at
(1904), 33, 168
Savino, Vincent, 135–36
Seaver, Walter, E., 83
Segal, Erich, 141–44
Semple, John D. (Jock), 97, 112–
16, 118, 150–51, 159–60
in shoving incident with Switzer
(1967), 93–96, 107–11, 113–
14, 189
Switzer given trophy by, 98
on women runners, 94, 97, 110,
114
Shakespeare, William, 21
Sheehan, George, 54

Shemin, Elias, 159, 160
Sherring, Bill, 166
Shigematsu, Morio, 165, 188
Shorter, Frank, 33, 191
Smith, Bernard Joseph, 164, 181
Sockalexis, Andrew, 170–71
S.P.C.A. (Society for the Prevention of Cruelty to Animals), 151
Spooner, O. Gardner, 15
Spring, Michael, 163, 167–68
Squires, Billy, 147, 155
Stamford (Connecticut), 7, 165
Stenroos, Albin, 33, 175
Stetson (college professor), 71
Stranahan, Frank, 58–59
Suomalainen, Olavi, 165, 190–91
Switzer, Katherine V., 93–111
  banned by Amateur Athletic Union (1968), 96, 109–10
  Briggs and, 103–6
  Cloney and, 107
  enters as "K. Switzer" (1967), 93–95, 106
  Semple gives trophy to, 98
  in shoving incident with Semple (1967), 93–96, 107–11, 113–14, 189
  as unofficial runner, 94–95, 106–9, 189

T

Tanaka, Shigeki, 164, 184
Task Force, 18–20
Tavares, Liz, 19
Tebeau Farm (Hopkinton), 14
Terasawa, Toru, 189

Timpany, Charles B., 161–62
Town Green (Hopkinton), 21
Trivoulidas, Peter, 164, 173
'Twas the Night Before Boston (Linscott), 110–11

U

Ullyot, Joan, 156
Unetani, Yoshiaki, 165, 190

V

Vandendriessche, Aurele, 165, 187–88
Ventrillo, Alfred, 137–40
Viskari, Antti, 164
Vogel, Ted, 85–86
  charges Cote with unfair tactics, 86, 183
Vrazanis, John, 167

W

Walter A. Brown School (Hopkinton), 13
Ward, Tom, 23
Watt, Geoffrey M., 15
Weiner, Sylvia, 17
Wellesley (Massachusetts), 21, 61, 62
Wheelchair competitors, 146–48
Wheelchair Marathon (Ohio), 147
Wick, Willie, 172

Wilson, Earl, 93
Windmill Point (Detroit), 132
Winter, Liane, 192
Wolde, Mamo, 34, 188
Women runners, 17, 49, 55, 92–
    97, 109, 156, 165, 189–92
  B.A.A. gives permission to com-
    pete to (1972), 93
  Collins on, 95
  dressing quarters for, 93, 110
  first unofficial participation by
    (1966), 92–93, 104
  Semple on, 94, 97, 110, 114
  world record time of (1975),
    192

Y

Yamada, Keizo, 164, 184
Yamamoto, Tomijii (U-6), 4–5
Yonkers (New York), 41
Young, Brigham, 12
Young, Walter, 164, 179, 180
Yun Bok Suh, 120, 150, 164, 182
Yun Chil Choi, 184

Z

Zatopek, Emil, 125
Zuna, F., 76, 164, 173, 174